LITERACY

How principals can support teachers and strengthen

LEADERSHIP

reading instruction in elementary classrooms

MATTERS

Karen Filewych

Pembroke Publishers Limited

© 2023 **Pembroke Publishers**
538 Hood Road
Markham, Ontario, Canada L3R 3K9
www.pembrokepublishers.com

Library and Archives Canada Cataloguing in Publication

Title: Literacy leadership matters : how principals can support teachers and strengthen reading instruction in elementary classrooms / Karen Filewych.

Names: Filewych, Karen, author.

Description: Includes bibliographical references and index.

Identifiers: Canadiana (print) 20220495521 | Canadiana (ebook) 20220495610 | ISBN 9781551383613 (softcover) | ISBN 9781551389615 (PDF)

Subjects: LCSH: Elementary school principals. | LCSH: Teacher-principal relationships. | LCSH: Educational leadership. | LCSH: Language arts (Elementary) | LCSH: Elementary school teachers—Training of.

Classification: LCC LB2831.9 .F55 2023 | DDC 371.2/011—dc23

Editor: Kat Mototsune
Cover Design: John Zehethofer
Typesetting: Jay Tee Graphics Ltd.

Printed and bound in Canada
9 8 7 6 5 4 3 2 1

Contents

Chapter 7: Writing   *80*

Chapter 8: Literacy in the Content Areas   *100*

Introduction: Instructional Leaders

"Leadership and learning are indispensable to each other."
— John F. Kennedy

Literacy Learning Before Our Eyes

It really is quite something! Dozens of five-year-olds enter our school—most of them non-readers and -writers, unable to make meaning from the markings on a page—and then, a few months and years of instruction later, they have become the newest members of our literate world. Sometimes it seems like it just happens, and yet our primary teachers understand the hard work and explicit instruction necessary each and every day to create these young readers and writers. Primary teachers know that literacy comes more easily to some than others. They know that sometimes they have to use every trick in the book, and that still some students struggle to grasp these oh-so-necessary skills. They also know that the more intentional and comprehensive the first years of literacy instruction, the more likely that students will celebrate success.

Entering the literate world is only the first step. Our students need continued quality literacy instruction throughout their elementary education. In order to teach literacy most effectively, it is important to understand the needs of the students before us, what is going on inside the brain, what the research demonstrates, and how the many pieces of the learning puzzle come together.

A Lack of Training

In the foreword to David Booth's book *The Literacy Principal*, Michael Fullan states, "If you had to name one thing that every school should do well, you would have to consider teaching deep literacy as standing head and shoulders over all other priorities. It is the key to every student's future." (7)

When we consider our own university education, how many teachers or administrators have more than a course or two in literacy instruction? Elementary generalists, maybe. The rest? Likely not. Yet many teachers find themselves teaching children to read and write, regardless of the grade level, and many administrators find themselves instructional leaders in an elementary school, regardless of their training—training which might very well be in secondary mathematics or science.

Leading an elementary school is notably different from leading either a junior high or high school. The first difference: size. A principal in an elementary school with a few hundred students will have a different role from that of a principal in a high school with thousands of students and a large staff. Another significant difference: structure and scope. In elementary schools, teachers typically teach most subjects to their students. A large part of their day includes targeted literacy instruction, not only within the language-arts classroom but also in other content areas. Literacy instruction in elementary school tends to underpin everything else we do! In junior high or high school, on the other hand, teachers typically specialize in one or two subject areas. Being a leader in these schools, then, is substantially different. A principal in an elementary school is often expected to be the instructional leader, whereas a principal in the high school down the street might not have these expectations placed upon them (a myriad of other expectations, though, of course). Leadership at one level is not inherently better or worse, or more important, than at the other, but we cannot deny the differences.

Leadership Demands and Questions

I have taught all elementary grade levels, worked as a language-arts consultant, and spent many years as an administrator. I thoroughly enjoyed each of these roles and found they challenged me in different ways. My experience in one role made me stronger in the others. One of the most important things I learned from being an administrator is that teachers want to feel heard and understood by their admin team. When in conversations with teachers, it helped that I could relate to them because I had taught the grade levels they were teaching. Yet I realize this is not always the reality. Because most school districts tend to have more elementary schools than junior high and high schools, often, when teachers of junior high and senior high move into administration, they are placed in an elementary school. This can be challenging when you don't have experience or an understanding of the elementary world. This is not said in judgment, purely in fact. If I was placed in a high school, I would have to work exceptionally hard at becoming an effective leader and relating to my staff because I was never a high-school teacher.

If elementary literacy is not your expertise, consider the impact of modelling your own learning journey with your staff. You will likely earn more respect if you admit that you are learning to be an instructional leader in literacy rather than if you present as though you fully understand the curriculum and the pedagogy supporting it.

In order to lead a school most effectively, we need to understand the many demands placed on our teachers, remember what it was like to be in the trenches, and find ways to support our teachers with their planning and instruction. If we want to build capacity with teachers and guide them in their teaching, it helps if we understand what it is they do. Sitting at one's desk, it is easy to get buried in the paperwork of managerial tasks and administrative duties. The duties are ones that must be attended to, yet the most effective leaders are those who are able to move beyond those tasks and connect with the *people* in their building: both staff and students.

In my work as a language-arts consultant, many administrators approached me with questions such as this: *How can I improve the reading instruction within my school? I have no background in literacy instruction, how do I know what my teachers should be doing as best practice when teaching reading and writing? I hear conflicting information about teaching reading. How do I know what to believe?*

This book is an attempt to provide answers to these questions. I have structured it in a way that I hope will make it an easy reference. Yes, read it all through once. But then return to specific topics as needed. If a question or dilemma arises—as they always do—my hope is that this book will provide some of the answers you're seeking.

Recurring Features to Support Your Practice

To support the professional learning and dialogue within your school, each chapter includes two recurring sections: Instructional Walk Considerations and Talk Time (a reproducible list of discussion ideas for staff meetings). Both sections are included by design, as I believe them to be foundational to instructional leadership. They are a way to better understand your teachers and the instruction going on in your school.

As a language-arts consultant, I provided a monthly newsletter for administrators and included sections similar to these. The feedback I received proved that they were used and helpful resources. I hope you find the same.

Instructional Walk Considerations

The Instructional Walk Considerations feature will provide you with specific things to look for as you walk the halls and classrooms of your school. These instructional walks are not meant to be evaluative or judgmental in nature. They are essential, though, for you to truly understand what is going on within your building. When I was an administrator, I found I had to schedule these instructional walks into my day. If not, the day disappeared and there I was, still at my desk with an ever-growing to-do list. It was one of my mentors who reminded me: if it's important, make time for it.

The time I spent in the classrooms and hallways of my school certainly helped me get to know our students. I tried to learn as many names as I could as a first step in building relationships. But I also wanted to be knowledgeable about what was going on in our classrooms. At first, this made some teachers uncomfortable. Some would stop teaching the moment I entered the classroom and not resume until I left, despite my indications to go on. Over time, most teachers understood my purpose and, although they might have stopped momentarily for the class to say a quick good morning, they would soon continue with the lesson.

Each grade level brings its own unique set of challenges and rewards. Kindergarten is an incredibly different beast from Grade 4, which, in turn, is different from a junior-high class and, again, a high-school class. This is true in terms of day-to-day routines and procedures, student needs, curricular focus, and, of course, literacy instruction. The Instructional Walk Considerations will give you something specific to look for and think about, ultimately leading to a better understanding of the current literacy instruction and needs within your school.

Talk Time

Talk Time encourages regular discussion with teachers—discussion about current practice, about pedagogy, about research. The reproducible will sometimes include a quotation from a prominent name in language learning, followed by questions to guide short discussion at staff meetings, discussion meant to help our teachers reflect on and improve their own practice. As we will discuss in Chapter 1, these conversations will not be as effective if we do not work together in an environment of trust. If teachers feel their practice is threatened, the discussion will not only be stilted, but also will be effectively meaningless. Our approach, then, is essential.

Staff meetings can sometimes be long and teachers are increasingly busy. These two truths can collide to create a difficult situation. We certainly don't want to

In *Read, Write, Lead*, Regie Routman (2014) describes this process: "In an instructional walk we are looking first for the teacher's strengths, noticing where support is needed, and also discerning instructional patterns across a school.... It is a process that respects both teacher and students. We are in the classroom to celebrate and support teachers, give positive feedback, move instruction forward, and increase the trust level between administrator and teachers across a school." (198)

add to the meeting length. When I was an assistant principal, the principal and I decided that anything that was informational in nature and did not require discussion would be sent as email. Our meeting time was saved for important instructional considerations and anything else for which discussion was warranted. Teachers appreciated this. The meetings felt purposeful and often positively influenced instruction. And, really, the meetings demonstrated what we as an admin team deemed most important and valued in our school.

In some chapters, multiple topics are presented for possible discussion with your teachers. Do not feel the need to use them all at once. Pick and choose those most relevant to your current context and group of teachers. The other ideas can always be used on another day. Deeper conversations about fewer questions are often more effective than surface conversations about many topics.

1

Creating a Shared Literacy Vision

"Leadership is the capacity to translate vision into reality."
— Warren Bennis

Leadership Matters

Strong leadership in a school is essential. Your role is essential. You set both the tone and the direction for what goes on within your building. I recently had a conversation about two schools with identical architectural blueprints. Despite having the same physical layout, these schools offered me two vastly different experiences. Why? Leadership. In one, the principal created an environment where everyone—students, staff, and guests—felt valued and welcome, where learning was exciting, and where everyone seemed willing to work hard. The other school was quite the opposite: feelings of mistrust, negativity, even judgment permeated the environment. Sadly, staff did not seem especially happy to be there. The identical buildings provided significantly different learning environments.

If we are to create an environment where literacy learning is valued by both staff and students, we must remember that our leadership matters. If we do not have experience or education with literacy instruction, knowing where to begin can be daunting. This chapter addresses important considerations to help with the creation of a shared literacy vision: approaching headlines about literacy instruction, creating an environment of trust, establishing common goals, focusing on pedagogy, using common language, reconsidering school-wide practices, building capacity, becoming literacy leaders in our schools, and finding the funds.

Fumbling Through the Headlines

One of the challenges of leading an elementary school, with the foundations of literacy at the core, is figuring out what makes literacy instruction most effective. You may have noticed an influx of headlines and news stories about reading instruction as of late. The term "the Science of Reading" is used with increasing frequency. Everyone seems to be weighing in on the argument about what is considered best practice for literacy instruction, especially when it comes to reading. The Ontario Human Rights Commission put out the *Right to Read* report. The Elementary Teachers' Federation of Ontario submitted an official response. Across the country, there have been significant curricular shifts in literacy instruction. The public debate has brought many stakeholders to the table with a varying amount of experience with, research into, and understanding of the topic. For elementary teachers who pride themselves in the teaching of reading, the conversation can sometimes feel personal, like an attack on their teaching.

In their book, *Shifting the Balance*, Jan Burkins and Kari Yates (2021) outline some of the current prevailing opinions:

> Some argue that there is a disconnect between research and classroom practice. Some argue that things are out of balance in the balanced literacy classroom. Still others argue that the methods in many classrooms are making learning to read harder rather than easier, especially for the children most at risk of reading difficulties. (1)

It can be challenging to keep up with what we hear and read, and also to make sense of it all.

Another term that is gaining popularity is *structured literacy*. As Louisa Moats (2020) explains,

> Recently, the International Dyslexia Association (IDA) adopted the term *Structured Literacy* to refer to the content and principles of explicit teaching that works best with students who must be taught how to read. (20)

Moats, a well-known researcher in the field, suggests that a more comprehensive term would be *Structured Language and Literacy* to acknowledge all components involved. She goes on to say,

> Ideally, a comprehensive program balances skill development with daily writing and reading that is purposeful and engaging. Reading and language instruction should occur within a rich, substantive, knowledge-building curriculum. (20)

As you will see throughout this book, this comprehensive program is what we strive for. A radical change of practice is likely not required in most classrooms. What is necessary, though? What is necessary is an attempt to understand the research and opportunities to reflect on and discuss current practice, leading to intentional adjustments to planning and instruction. The intent of this book is to guide you and your staff through this process.

Creating an Environment of Trust

The teaching of reading often brings with it long-held and passionate beliefs of teachers. Some teachers are quite confident in their methods. On the other hand, there are some teachers who feel insecure about teaching reading because of the limited coursework they received on the topic. Because of these realities, as administrators or literacy leads, we are not wise to abruptly enter the conversation and impose our own learnings or beliefs. Doing so could well accomplish the opposite of what we intend. Instead, the dialogue surrounding these

Just like the students in our classrooms, our teachers have their own strengths and challenges, understandings and experiences. We cannot make assumptions that every elementary teacher has the tools necessary to teach language arts with expertise; teachers often do not want to reveal their weaknesses, especially to their administrators.

"The gardener does not make a plant grow. The job of a gardener is to create optimal conditions."
—Sir Ken Robinson

"Leaders need first to take on the role of supportive coach before taking on the role of evaluator." (Routman 2014, 199)

Writing notes to your staff may not be your preference. Consider your strengths and your end goal. What will you do to establish trust and show that you value your staff, as colleagues and as people?

topics should be open, intentional, reflective, and collaborative. This is much more easily accomplished in an environment of trust. If our teachers feel like we are dictating what is to be done—which might be contrary to what they've done for years—we will likely encounter resistance. Instead, consider how you might embark together on this learning journey to improve literacy instruction: sharing research, asking questions, and inviting collaboration, respecting all voices at the table.

In most books, blog posts, or courses about leadership, there is a focus on building a community of respect and trust. We recognize the importance of this environment if we are going to be successful in working toward common goals. Yet this environment is not always an easy one to create. Effective leaders know that to accomplish the big things, they have to be intentional about the little things along the way: a painter has a vision of the end creation but must focus on each small detail to create the overall effect.

My former colleagues have told me that it was one of the little things I did as an administrator that had the biggest impact on them. I wrote short notes acknowledging something I noticed in their classrooms—a stunning bulletin board, a gentle manner with a challenging student, excellent classroom management, an intriguing lesson—and left the notes in their mailboxes. By doing this, I was recognizing their strengths, and I was building community in the process. Teachers appreciated this and many mentioned that they saved my notes over the years. This simple practice helped teachers understand the purpose of my instructional walks, developed strong relationships, and made future conversations about anything from challenging students to classroom instruction much easier.

I was intentional about these notes. In fact, I kept a staff list at my desk. Every week I would try to write five or six notes, working my way through the staff list. I didn't start at the top and work my way down; I completed the list organically. As I noticed something in a particular class or with a particular staff member, I would write that note and check the name off my list. When everyone had one note, I would start again. My staff didn't know how intentional this was. The list on my desk not only reminded me to write the notes but also ensured that I wrote something to everyone. I also tried to be attentive to the circumstances and needs of my staff. If I knew someone was having a tough week (because of a challenge in school or a home circumstance), that individual would be sure to get a note. Writing these notes was a little thing to me, but perhaps it was a big thing to that person in that moment.

As a teacher, I have worked on school staffs where I felt valued as a teacher and where I know others felt valued in their roles, too. In these situations, productivity and motivation were high, and everyone was willing to put in the extra effort because we felt valued. Professional reading and discussion? Absolutely. We saw the benefit for our students and were willing to take the time and make the effort to learn and improve our instruction.

In their uplifting book, *Dear Teacher*, Brad Johnson and Hal Bowman (2021) say this to teachers:

> While you do have high expectations for your students and want them to give their best, remember that they are human first, and when you focus on things like building relationships and patience, they will actually work harder and be more successful. Students work harder for teachers they like and who like them. (3)

The same holds true for you and your teachers. Building relationships, valuing the gifts of those on your staff, respecting them as human beings, remembering that they have lives outside of school, and creating a community of trust are essential. The little things—okay, maybe they're not so little—enable us to create common goals and have meaningful conversations about best practice, ultimately leading toward our larger goal of effective literacy instruction, affecting our students' lives forever.

Establishing Common Goals

At the beginning of the school year, I ask teachers their goals for the year. Some schools (or school districts) require this formally of their teachers; however, the reflection and dialogue around goal-setting can also be accomplished informally in the setting of a staff meeting. In elementary schools, almost every teacher mentions—unprompted—something about their students as readers and/or writers. I would be concerned if they didn't; after all, literacy instruction is vital in our elementary classrooms.

Most school districts require schools to outline their goals for the year (and the strategies they plan to use to meet those goals). Before deciding on your school goals, facilitate a conversation about teacher goals first. That discussion will naturally feed into the conversation about school goals. If your school district outlines specific areas for you to target (equity and inclusion, for example), these areas can then be discussed as they relate to the goals of your teachers.

Administrators have sometimes asked me to assist them in creating their literacy goals. My suggestion is always to consider both staff observations about students and the data from previous years. Data is often the driving force of our goals and also how we measure success. When creating your literacy goals and the strategies you will implement, consider the specific needs within your school.

See the Glossary on page 127 for words in bold print.

- Does your data show that students are competent at decoding but need more support with comprehension?
- Are there an inordinate number of students requiring literacy intervention?
- Do you see the need for more intentional teaching of **phonological awareness** and **phonemic awareness**?
- Have you been successful in improving student reading but now need a more intentional focus on writing?
- Does your staff have the resources needed to implement your goals?

In my experience, it is more effective to target one or two specific areas than to write a broad goal and try to accomplish everything all at once. A goal like *To improve student achievement in reading, writing, speaking, and listening* is broad in scope and could be difficult to track and achieve, not to mention being overwhelming for teachers. Instead, it might be more manageable and more effective to target one area. Will this area affect the others? Likely. But keep the goal targeted and specific. This chapter's Talk Time on page 19 could support you in goal-setting with your staff.

Focusing on Pedagogy

If literacy underpins all we do in our elementary classrooms, we should be talking about literacy instruction regularly. We move toward what we focus on. By setting aside time for this discussion, it shows what we value in our school. When planning your staff meetings, consider choosing questions from Talk Time one chapter at a time, one element of language learning at a time. This will ensure your discussion is guided and grounded in pedagogy.

Although I have structured this book by separating the various elements of language learning, it is essential that we—and our teachers—realize that these elements are very much interconnected. (We will discuss this more in Chapter 2.) They are so interconnected, in fact, that it was sometimes difficult to decide which topics should be in which chapter. As an example, should phonemic awareness be in the chapter on word study or reading? One could make an argument for both. Therefore, if you are looking for a specific topic, check the contents or index. Otherwise, you might decide to work through the discussion questions one chapter at a time.

You'll notice that the heading for this section refers to pedagogy and not curriculum. The difference between the two? Curriculum is *what* is being taught and pedagogy refers to *how*. Although curriculum is an important part of the conversation, the discussion should most often focus on pedagogy: *how* we are teaching the curriculum to maximize student learning.

Using Common Language

Now that I am no longer working for one school division, schools often hire me as a writer-in-residence. One of the most effective outcomes of this experience is building common language for all students and teachers within the school. This is also something you will accomplish through regular staff meeting discussions about pedagogy. Common language is powerful when we, as a staff, are discussing our vision, our goals, and our practice. Common language in the classroom can also propel our students' learning forward as they move from grade to grade.

The language-arts curriculum is known as a spiral curriculum: a concept is revisited repeatedly from year to year, with complexity increasing and student understanding deepening. In essence, we are building on what we have learned in previous years, rather than introducing new content and concepts each year. Using common language, then, helps students see the connections in what they are being taught, rather than leaving them feeling like teachers are continually introducing new concepts.

(Re)Considering School-wide Practices

Sometimes when we develop a common understanding, common goals, and common language with our teachers, we decide to establish school-wide literacy practices. If well thought-out, school-wide practices can improve both the practice of our teachers and the learning for our students. However, we must be cautious about becoming overzealous and implementing something just for the sake of implementation.

Let's consider a few examples. Many schools implement a school-wide period of time for independent reading: fifteen minutes each day when everyone is reading, for example. In *Sometimes Reading is Hard*, Robin Bright (2021) suggests,

> Fifteen minutes is magic!… Carving out 15 minutes a day can make all the difference. That length of time is considered consequential in helping students improve their decoding, fluency, vocabulary, and comprehension reading skills. And it's so easy to make this a part of your daily routine. (85)

A few considerations: What time of day is best for most classrooms? How will we ensure students are actually engaged in reading? What should students be reading at this time? What are teachers doing during independent reading? (These questions will be addressed in Chapter 6.)

As a school-wide practice, my preference is to begin the day with independent reading. In some schools with a morning broadcast or announcements, I have noticed a surprising amount of wasted instructional time, as nothing consequential occurs in the classroom until those announcements begin. And yet, let's think about how purposeful this time could be. Take those 15 minutes and multiply them by 5 days in a week: 75 minutes a week! Let's assume a 40-week school year: 75 minutes multiplied by 40 equals 3000 minutes. That's 50 hours of reading or instruction that our students are missing out on! If we establish the first 15 minutes of class as independent reading time—and we ensure that announcements or broadcast occur consistently at the same time each day—this instructional time becomes purposeful, rather than time spent waiting.

Let's consider another example of a school-wide practice: An elementary school implemented school-wide, multi-grade literacy groupings for 90 minutes every morning (three 30-minute blocks). All available staff were used to work with students in small groups. Students moved from adult to adult during those three blocks of time to work on different skills and strategies; teachers, then, did not always work with their own students. Although this plan was well-intentioned, many teachers said they did not feel the time was as valuable as it could have been. For one thing, they were not able to plan as well for these groupings as they could for their own class. Other teachers said that the time spent transitioning in and out of the groupings was neither efficient nor productive, often leaving three 20- or 25-minute blocks rather than using all 30 minutes with each group. So, although the intention of the admin team was commendable (and the planning considerable), many of the teachers resented this practice and felt that it was infringing on the quality instructional time they had with their own students.

If you are thinking about implementing a school-wide practice, or if there is currently a school-wide practice in place, consider these questions:

- What is the desired outcome?
- Will this practice use instructional time effectively?
- Is time used efficiently or is a lot of time spent in transitions? Is it an easy-to-implement practice?
- Will this practice improve student learning?
- When will we schedule time to talk about this practice as a staff to hear how it is working or not working?
- How might you generate excitement and a buy-in from your staff?

In *The Book Whisperer*, Donalyn Miller (2009) says, "The question can no longer be 'How can we make time for independent reading?' The question must be 'How can we not?'" (51)

Building Capacity

I once read that the best leaders are people who feel great about themselves. I have given this statement a lot of thought and considered it in regard to the leaders I have worked with. Perhaps it holds some truth. The most effective leaders I know are those who understand that they aren't necessarily the smartest in the room, who don't try to do everything themselves, who know the value of team, and who build others up while capitalizing on their unique gifts. If you are a secondary-trained principal leading an elementary school, this is confirmation that you can be an effective administrator in this environment even though you might feel out of your comfort zone.

The fact that you're reading this book shows a willingness to learn and improve. As you consider how to proceed with literacy goals within your school, think carefully about how you can build capacity and empower your staff, capitalizing on the strengths of your team to create the biggest impact.

Becoming Literacy Leaders in Our Schools

One of the unofficial goals in most elementary schools is to inspire a love of reading. What students see around them should promote a love of reading, invite students to read, and demonstrate how the adults in the school are readers too! Are there nooks with books throughout your school? Are the books within your students' reach? Are there books on display with the covers visible (not only the spines)? Do the book displays change regularly? Are there child-friendly quotes around the building? Bulletin boards to show favorite books of staff members? The physical environment within a school speaks volumes. What do you want your space to say?

The most effective literacy teachers are those who value reading and ensure they are reading what their students are reading. These teachers can easily recommend books to their students and engage in meaningful conversations. And yet this is something administrators don't often think to do. Imagine the immediate connection you could make with a class if you asked them for a book recommendation, borrowed the book, and then returned the following week to share your reaction. Students who hadn't yet read the book would be much more likely to pick it up, knowing that their principal had read it too! Do you have young children or grandchildren in your life? Visit your primary classes and ask students for recommendations. They will be thrilled to tell you about their favorite books. The best part? This excitement is contagious. Students who haven't had much exposure to books at home, or students whose feelings about books have been primarily ones of frustration, in time may be influenced by the interest you show and by these positive associations with books.

Do you give out birthday pencils or certificates to the students in your school? Is there any way you could give books instead? I know of many schools who have creatively found the funds to purchase a wide variety of books; on their birthdays, students choose from this selection. I have witnessed many students skipping down the hall with a new book of their own—a gift of literacy in more ways than one!

The bottom line: don't leave it to your teachers to be the only literacy leaders in your school. How can you become a literacy leader for students too?

Finding the Funds

As principal, one of the challenges you face continually is budget. Whether we realize it or not, financial decisions are revealing and reflect what is valued within a school. If you believe strongly in the importance of literacy within your building, do your financial decisions demonstrate this? Are you committed to purchasing the resources needed to support your school goals? Have you allocated some of your budget to pay for a librarian or teacher librarian, even on a part-time basis? Have you set aside funds to support literacy school-wide, such as creating an environment to promote a love of reading?

Financial decisions that support literacy demonstrate what you value: to students, to staff, to parents. Money talks.

When budgets are especially tight, get creative. Pursue additional funding through grant applications. Be open to book donations (perhaps from a more affluent school or from the public library that might be culling). Consider: Are the book donations suitable for your library or could they be donated to families in need? In what ways can your school council support your literacy goals?

Instructional Walk Considerations: A Shared Literacy Vision

On your next instructional walk, consider:

- What do you notice about the physical environment of your school? Does it reflect the importance of literacy and promote a love of reading?
- Look at your school through the eyes of a student. What might they notice to help them understand that literacy is valued in their school?
- What might you do to improve the physical space to ensure that it reflects your core beliefs and your school goals?
- Are school-wide interruptions (announcements, phone calls to the classroom, pages for the principal to come to the office) kept to a minimum to protect instructional time? How can you ensure that communication does not negatively affect learning and teaching?
- What are the strengths of the teachers within your school?
- Is there a school-wide practice already in place within your school? If so, does it seem to be effective? Does it honor instructional time?
- What are your students reading? What books do they recommend to you?
- How might you facilitate the sharing of student book recommendations with other students in the school? On a school-wide bulletin board? Through a book talk during broadcast?

Talk Time: A Shared Literacy Vision

Take some time to read and think about this quotation and these questions before discussing them with your colleagues.

In *The 7 Habits of Highly Effective People*, Stephen Covey (2004) said, "To begin with the end in mind means to start with a clear understanding of your destination. It means to know where you're going so that you better understand where you are now and so that the steps you take are always in the right direction." (98)

- How does this quote apply to your work with students?
- What are your goals for your students this year? (Prioritize 3 or 4 at most.)
- What do you plan to do to reach these goals? Be specific.
- Which of your goals might be appropriate to consider as part of our school goals? Is there a way we can work toward one of these goals collectively as a staff?

Other questions for discussion:
- Think about your classroom environment. Does it reflect your own personal goals for the year or your school-wide literacy goal(s)? Is there anything you might add or change?
- What do you suggest we do to our school environment to better reflect our literacy goals?

Pembroke Publishers ©2023 *Literacy Leadership Matters* by Karen Filewych ISBN 978-1-55138-361-3

2

The Role of Language in Our Classrooms

"The limits of your language are the limits of your world."
— Ludwig Wittgenstein

The Nature of Language

Imagine your day without language. It's hard to do. Each and every moment of the day—whether we are conscious of it or not—language is at work for all of us.

How might you demonstrate or emphasize the three purposes of language—thinking, communicating, and learning—within your staff meetings?

The front matter of the Alberta English Language Arts and Literature curriculum (2022) says, "Language is a uniquely structured system that forms the basis for thinking, communicating, and learning." Consider each of these: *thinking, communicating,* and *learning*. We *think* through language. We *communicate* through language. We *learn* through language. It might sound monotonous here, but this point is worth repeating. When I have asked teachers to explain the purpose of language, most respond with "communication." As educators, though, we should be cognizant of how *thinking* and *learning* are also accomplished through language. In fact, these two purposes of language should be at the forefront of our minds as we plan our instruction.

See the Glossary on page 127 for words in bold print.

Language is divided into six strands: listening and speaking, reading and writing, viewing and representing. Young children begin with listening and viewing, of course; over time, they develop the other strands of language as well. All six strands are interconnected. Within each strand of language, there are various elements necessary for us to understand and teach our students: these elements form the basis of our language-arts curriculum. Within the strand of reading, for example, we explicitly teach **phonetic decoding**, fluency, vocabulary, and comprehension. And within each of those elements of reading, there are other specifics that our students must learn. What about grammar and **morphology**, syntax and semantics? No wonder the teaching of literacy is so complex!

The Organization of This Book

In order to write this book, I had to decide on an organizational structure. After much consideration, I decided to break the chapters into the various elements of language arts at work in our classrooms. Inherent in this approach is the danger of the reader interpreting these elements as existing separately from one another, in silos. In actuality, the strands of language (and the elements within each strand) should always be working together. One strand sometimes takes a leading role during a lesson and the others exist in supporting roles. In another lesson, one of the other strands of language would take the leading role, which would cause the supporting roles to shift.

Let's suppose a teacher invites you into the classroom to observe a lesson on writing. While observing this lesson where writing takes the leading role, watch for the other strands of language in supporting roles. An effective teacher will be reading and referring to mentor texts, exploring the craft of authors, discussing words and word study, and using oral language throughout. The more intentionally they do this, the better.

Just as I caution you about isolating my chapters from one another, I also caution teachers about isolating the components of language arts. For example, the most recent English Language Arts and Literature curriculum in Alberta is divided into these Organizing Ideas: Text Forms and Structures, Oral Language, Vocabulary, Phonological Awareness, Phonics, Fluency, Comprehension, Writing, and Conventions. A Guiding Question followed by specific outcomes are included under each of these Organizing Ideas. The intent is not to teach them separately. For ease of reading and understanding, they are divided. In our classrooms, they should not be.

Language at Work in Our Classrooms

Consider teaching anything without language. Could you do it?

All six strands of language—listening, speaking, reading, writing, viewing, and representing—are at work throughout the day, regardless of the subject area we happen to be teaching. Although language arts is one curricular area, the most effective elementary teachers are deliberate in how they use language in the classroom and cognizant of the role that language plays in thinking, communicating, and learning. The most effective teachers are those who deliberately integrate language learning into all curricular areas. This reflects strong pedagogy. Let's examine a couple of scenarios.

> After teaching a lesson in social studies about democracy, the teacher asks the class a question to check for understanding. A student in the front of the class raises a hand immediately. The teacher invites that student to respond. The student responds, and the teacher moves on, pleased there was understanding of the content.
>
> I'm sure you see what's wrong with this scenario. Yes, that one student demonstrated an understanding of the content. In fact, there's a good chance that this particular student grasps most content quickly. The other students in the class likely realize that this student can be counted on to respond to the teacher's questions. In

As you observe teachers and students, consider how language is used to *think, communicate*, and *learn*. How might you bring more awareness of these roles of language within your school?

effect, the other students don't even have to process the question (think) or consider how to articulate an answer (communicate), knowing that this other student will probably respond. This teacher has inadvertently removed the thinking, communicating, and perhaps even the learning for many of the students in the class.

A few slight shifts in this process can ensure that all students are thinking about the questions being asked. To begin, the teacher can increase the wait time after asking the question and intentionally ask each student to formulate an answer. Then, after a minute or two, students can turn and discuss their answers with a partner; this ensures that all students are given the opportunity to articulate their thinking and communicate with another individual, ultimately helping them process their learning. If this becomes routine, students will know that they are all expected to think about the question, formulate an answer, and then communicate that answer. Not one student. All students. After the turn-and-talk, the teacher could still ask someone to share with the whole class but, by this point, everyone has been involved in the learning.

Today in Grade 2, it is time for students to test the boats they have built! They put each boat on the water, adding weight to test its durability and strength. Students cheer or commiserate about the results and then they move on to the next boat. After all boats are tested, the bell dismisses the students for recess. When they re-enter the classroom, they move on to a lesson in math.

Again, the problem with this approach is fairly obvious. Presumably, the purpose of building the boats is that students understand the principles related to floating, test various materials and designs, and then create a boat based on their learning. Testing the boats is an important part of the process. The intentional use of language, however, would certainly enhance the thinking and learning of the students. What if, after all students had the opportunity to test their boats, they spent 6 to 7 minutes freewriting about what they noticed? Every student would then be writing down their thoughts and observations, consolidating their learning and constructing meaning from the experience. After the freewrite, the teacher could invite students to share their writing with the class. The teacher would then gain insight into the students' learning and possibly realize some misconceptions, discovering that further discussion or teaching is required, or maybe feeling confident that the students have grasped the concepts. Either way, adding the freewrite to the lesson does not take much time, yet the learning experience becomes more effective for both students and teacher.

Thinking about these specific scenarios is enlightening. The explicit teaching of the lessons might have been stellar; however, without consideration of the role of language within learning, students may not have had the opportunity to process what was being taught or consolidate their learning. The opportunities for reflection, articulation of their thinking, and writing will also help with long-term retention.

So although the subject area of language arts is where students learn how to use language in many forms and contexts, you can see that language itself is at work every moment of the day.

When I was observing a teacher in the classroom for evaluation purposes, I would ask these questions during our debrief afterwards: *What do you think went well?* and *What might you do differently next time?* Once the teacher shared their own answers to these questions, I would then share my answers to the same questions, all in the spirit of growth. For example, during your observation, you might have noticed the teacher intentionally using various strands of language to deepen student understanding. Or you might have noticed that this strategy was not used by the teacher during the lesson. Either way, it is worth commenting on during the debrief, to confirm what was done well or to suggest a way to strengthen the lesson.

Writing as a Form of Thinking: Low-Stakes Writing

If you know my other teacher resources, you likely know about freewriting. In my first book *How Do I Get Them to Write?* I included a chapter about this powerful process in elementary classrooms. The response to that book, and to freewriting in particular, led to the writing and publication of my second book *Freewriting with Purpose*, in which I discuss in detail how this form of writing can be used across the curriculum. I whole-heartedly believe in the process.

Students should be writing in our classrooms daily. Sometimes when I say this, teachers at first interpret this in a different way from what I intend and become overwhelmed. But it is crucial to remember that the type of writing is important. If our students were writing formal assignments daily, assignments that they knew would be assessed, this would be considered *high-stakes* writing. On the other hand, if our students are writing regularly, using writing as a form of thinking—as reader response, as a reaction to a science experiment, as reflection—this is considered *low-stakes* writing. This is the type of writing we want to see more regularly in our classrooms. Not only will our students gain writing practice, but they will also have the opportunity to think through the page and strengthen their learning in all areas of study!

Should we ever assess our students' writing? Of course, but in moderation and with intention. Our elementary students should have many opportunities to practice their writing, for many purposes and in many forms, rather than only written assignments that will be assessed. (More on this in Chapter 7!)

Watch for Meaningful Talk

In *Literacy Essentials*, Routman (2018) says, "Productive and collaborative talk increases engagement, helps clarify meaning, improves retention of information, shapes and improves thinking capacities, leads to deeper understanding, and results in more enduring learning." (153–154)

Silent classrooms are sometimes interpreted to be engaged, well-managed, and compliant classrooms. Yet knowing what we do about the nature of language, we see this isn't always the case. Is there a time for a silent classroom? Absolutely. My classroom would likely be fairly quiet during independent reading, and during freewriting, too. But a quiet classroom is certainly not something we want to strive for all day long. For much of the day, we should purposefully give our students opportunities to talk: to articulate their thinking, share opinions, ask questions, and communicate their learning.

John Hattie is known for his work on *visible learning*. There is an extensive visible learning data base and many factors have been studied to determine various effects on learning. In *Teaching Literacy in the Visible Learning Classroom*, Fisher, Frey, and Hattie (2017) reference Hattie's research:

Let's consider increasing classroom discourse (synonymous with classroom discussion or dialogue). Students would be invited to talk with their peers in collaborative groups, working to solve complex and rich tasks…. The effect size of classroom discourse is 0.82, well above our threshold, and likely to result in two years of learning gains for a year of schooling. (3)

According to Hattie, this effect size is in the high range, and demonstrates how students will benefit from opportunities to participate in meaningful talk.

Just as we are wary of the silent classroom, we should also be wary of classrooms where a small group of students dominate the talk. If we pay close attention during teacher-led discussion, we might find it is often only three or four students who contribute. But by using strategies like turn-and-talk or other cooperative learning structures, all students have the opportunity to construct meaning and share their thinking. As Hattie's research demonstrates, this will greatly improve student learning.

On your next instruction walk, be intentional about observing the talk occurring within your classrooms. Who is doing the talking? Is the talk purposeful? Does the teacher provide opportunities for all students to articulate their thinking? Consider what you see over time rather than making assumptions based on one observation.

The Importance of Viewing in Today's World

Our students are constantly surrounded by information and text in the form of images and videos, which include features such as graphics, sound, animations, and various designs. Text has a broader meaning than ever before: songs, artifacts, dance, buildings, rituals, paintings, multi-media experiences, and much more. Never has it been more important for our students to become discerning, critical-thinking viewers of information.

Sometimes we may wonder about teacher requests for specific resources. Perhaps they are exposing students to a variety of text types. Ask questions to better understand teacher intentions.

My last trip to the movie theatre reminded me of the number of messages and the varied intent of the messages that our students encounter on a daily basis. Before the movie, there were movie clips and trivia questions about the movies, the characters, and the actors. Then there were countless commercials that we would previously have expected to see only on TV. Next there were three or four movie previews before the feature presentation. When you think about it, even though they were all in video form, these representations had different formats, styles, biases, and intents. Helping students understand the elements of whatever it is they are viewing is essential in helping them understand the messages themselves.

In our classrooms, therefore, we should be intentional about providing our students with various forms of text to view and discuss. This can help students become more critical and discerning viewers of information.

What Do We Mean by *Representing*?

When discussing the six strands of language, teachers often ask about representing. What is it and why is it important?

If you see students in the hallway working on some form of representation, ask what they are doing and why. Give them an opportunity to articulate the process to you!

We are all unique as learners. Some individuals feel less confident representing ideas in words and more confident expressing ideas in other forms. Both forms of expression—in words and otherwise—are important, and one should not be at the expense of the other. But consider how representing ideas through charts, diagrams, movements, gestures, sounds, models, images, posters, video presentations, dramatizations, or music could be another way to make sense of our learning. Some forms are more suitable to certain situations or content. But what I love about this strand of language is that creativity and personal style often shine through.

I have been in situations where I have been asked to represent my learning in some way. Sometimes this feels daunting, especially if it is left open-ended. And yet the thinking required to decide on an appropriate representation—form and content—is powerful. Often metaphors develop through the process of representation. They don't have to, but they often do.

This strand of language can deepen our students' understanding and learning about a topic. Keep in mind that representation doesn't always have to be on a large scale or complex in nature. Sometimes it might simply be the opportunity to "use pictures and words to draw your understanding of today's science lesson." The more often students are asked to represent their learning in various ways, the more confident they become.

Giving Students Awareness of the Purpose of Language

Good pedagogy capitalizes on using language intentionally. Ideally, though, we also want students to understand how they use language to communicate, to think, and to learn. The idea of metacognition—thinking about one's thinking—helps us become more aware of ourselves as learners. This process is a higher-level skill that can have impact on future learning. I ensure that the role of language is also part of this conversation. After all, when we are aware of ourselves as learners, we can make informed decisions about when (and why) to use a particular strategy. When we are aware of how we use language within our learning, we can become much more intentional about the process. You can model this process with teachers through opportunities for reflection and metacognition during staff meetings and professional learning opportunities.

If you were to observe me in a classroom, you would often see me thinking aloud. My students know why I am teaching what I am teaching. But they also hear how I use language to problem-solve and make decisions. During a read-aloud, I might think aloud to demonstrate how I break apart an unfamiliar word to figure out its meaning. During a shared writing experience, I might think aloud so my students can see and hear my thought process about the organization of my ideas.

With students, I talk openly and often about the role of language in our learning.

- When and where do we read? Why is reading important?
- What types of text do you enjoy reading? What types of text do you find more challenging?
- Did your understanding of this text change after you talked to your group? Why do you think that is?
- What did you notice about your freewrite today? Did your thinking change? Do you think you would have come to this realization without freewriting?
- What helps you understand and remember what we are learning in class?
- When you are asked to represent your learning, what forms of representation do you gravitate toward? Why do you think that is?

"When teaching and learning are visible, there is a greater likelihood of students reaching higher levels of achievement." — John Hattie

Would it be helpful for you to understand your teachers as learners? Their preferences, challenges, and strengths? This becomes a purposeful reason to model questions about the role of language in learning during staff meetings.

- What goals do you have for yourself as a learner this month? What strategies are you going to use to help your learning? Think about the role of language and how you learn best.

Instructional Walk Considerations: The Nature of Language

After reading and thinking more about the nature of language, consider these questions on your next instructional walk:

- Are teachers being intentional about the use of language in their classrooms?
- Do students (at all grade levels) have the opportunity to talk regularly to articulate their thinking, share opinions, and construct meaning?
- Does the structure in the classroom enable all students to answer questions or do only a handful of students answer during discussion? (Keep an eye out for structures such as these: turn-and-talk, inside/outside circle, two lines, Kagan cooperative learning strategies.)
- What practices do you see in place that support learning within your school?
- If you are secondary-trained or new to an elementary school, do you notice any practices that are different from those used with older students? Any that are similar?

Talk Time: Language in Your Classrooms

Take some time to read and think about these quotations and questions before discussing them with your colleagues.

All six strands of language—listening, speaking, reading, writing, viewing, and representing—are at work throughout the day regardless of the subject area we happen to be teaching.

In *Literacy Essentials*, Routman (2018) says,

> Productive and collaborative talk increases engagement, helps clarify meaning, improves retention of information, shapes and improves thinking capacities, leads to deeper understanding, and results in more enduring learning. (153–154)

- How do you intentionally use language to improve learning within your classroom?
- Are there any strands of language that you unintentionally neglect? How might you change this?
- What strategies do you use to ensure that *all* your students, not just a select few, have the opportunity to talk?
- Are your students thinking and talking about their learning each day?
- Do you explain to your students why you do what you do?
- Do you use think-alouds so your students can hear your process?

Pembroke Publishers ©2023 *Literacy Leadership Matters* by Karen Filewych ISBN 978-1-55138-361-3

3

Planning and Resources

"I hear and I forget. I see and I remember. I do and I understand."
— Confucius

In my work as a language-arts consultant, the most common question seemed to be "Where do I begin?" Unlike in other subject areas, there is nothing linear about teaching language arts. It is not broken into content-area topics. There is no one resource. There is not one textbook or set of lessons to follow. For many, especially those without specific courses in the teaching of language arts, this is simply overwhelming. Not to mention that other noteworthy questions often arise:

- "How do I teach children to read?"
- "What about writing? I have no idea how to teach writing."
- "What's the difference between **phonics** and **phonological awareness**? And how do I teach them to my students?"
- "Morphology? What's that?"

We will get into the specifics of these elements in the upcoming chapters, to give you a firm understanding of each in order to support your teachers. First things first, though: let's talk planning. This becomes the foundation for everything else in our language-arts classrooms and is often something teachers of language arts find particularly challenging. As an administrator, you will not likely be planning to teach language arts. However, it is important to understand the challenges faced by your teachers and also what makes for strong instruction.

In *Visible Learning for Teachers: Maximizing Impact on Learning*, John Hattie (2012) says,

School leaders and teachers need to create schools, staffrooms, and classroom environments in which error is welcomed as a learning opportunity, in which discarding incorrect knowledge and understandings is welcomed, and in which teachers can feel safe to learn, re-learn, and explore knowledge and understanding. (19)

The environment of trust that we spoke of in Chapter 1 is vital if our teachers are going to feel safe enough to take risks and engage in meaningful discussions with their colleagues about shifts in planning and instruction.

The Gradual Release of Responsibility

I can't write about planning or instruction in the classroom (or give an in-service session, it seems) without discussing the *gradual release of responsibility,* a term coined by Pearson and Gallagher in 1983. This pedagogical model begins with *explicit instruction,* moves to *guided instruction,* to *collaborative practice,* and eventually to *independent practice.* The gradual release of responsibility ensures that students have the scaffolding required to support their learning. When I studied the gradual release of responsibility during my undergraduate degree, the concept seemed abstract; I certainly did not understand its importance or the impact it would have on my teaching. If you are familiar with the work of Vygotsky and Piaget, you will recognize their influence in this model.

I Do	*We Do*	*You Do It Together*	*You Do It Alone*
Explicit Instruction	Guided Instruction	Collaborative Practice (without teacher guidance)	Independent Practice
teacher as **model**	teacher as **guide**	teacher as **resource**	teacher as **observer**
Gradual Release of Responsibility			

As a beginning teacher (like many teachers, I assume), I was fairly good at explicit instruction, but I expected my students to immediately demonstrate their understanding of the content or skills I was teaching. And I wondered why they couldn't! When I revisited the gradual release of responsibility and thought about the theory in relation to the real beings in front of me, I realized the importance of scaffolded practice to ensure student success. The difference it made to student learning and understanding was incredible. Thinking about my planning and instruction in this way transformed my teaching.

The gradual release of responsibility is typically more explicit and more common in our elementary classrooms than in junior high and high school. What should you watch for? Sometimes, teachers will work through the gradual release of responsibility within one lesson. Often, though—especially in elementary language arts—teachers work through the gradual release more deeply over the course of the week. Regardless of the timeline, watch for the four stages as illustrated in the chart above and outlined specifically here.

Explicit Instruction: *I do*

In *Visible Learning for Literacy*, Fisher, Frey, and Hattie (2016) remind us, "Learning becomes more meaningful when learners see what they're learning as being meaningful in their own lives." (112)

Direct, intentional instruction provides students with the know-how and the how-to that they need to master a skill or strategy on their own. In our elementary classrooms, this explicit instruction is best accomplished through short, intentional mini-lessons. Often mini-lessons are only 10 to 20 minutes in length, depending on what is being taught. Teachers should be clear about the learning intentions (the what and the why) for their mini-lessons; they can make these intentions clear to students, too.

Let's explore a Grade 1 example of explicit instruction related to phonics. This example can provide a glimpse of what you might see in your primary classrooms.

1. Before anything else, I state the learning intention—the what and the why:

   Today we are going to learn how some letters come together to make a new sound. This is going to help us when we are reading and when we are writing!

2. Then I begin with the explicit teaching:

   What does an s say? You're right! /s/ What does an h say? Right again, /h/ But when we see s and h together, they do not say /s//h/. Together they make the new sound /sh/. Try it with me. /sh/.

For clarity, letters or letter combinations (**graphemes**) are indicated with italics: *sh*. Here I would say the names of the letters. Sounds (**phonemes**) are indicated by backslashes: /sh/. Here I would say the sound made by those letters.

3. I would then continue with an interactive read-aloud, in which I read to students and explicitly highlight and discuss words with *sh*. This practice ensures that this phonics concept is not taught in isolation but rather in a real context that students will encounter. (Depending on the level of the class, I might decide to focus on words that begin with *sh*; however, if my class seems ready, I could also introduce words with *sh* in the middle or at the end of a word.)

4. During this mini-lesson, I would also show students how knowing *sh* will help with our writing. I would demonstrate writing words with the grapheme *sh*, modelling the **segmenting** of sounds as I go:

   Grade Ones, knowing that sh says /sh/ can also help us with our writing! Watch as I spell the word ship. The first sound I hear in ship is /sh/. Now we know that sh says /sh/ so I can print sh. The next sound I hear is /i/. We know that an i says /i/ so I will print an i. I will say the word again: ship. The last sound I hear in ship is /p/. I know a p says /p/. Read the word with me: ship.

Timothy Shanahan once said, "Never do with a small group, what could be done as well with the whole class." Do your teachers capitalize on whole-class instruction?

When we consider this example, it becomes clear why explicit instruction is necessary. How would a student discover this concept without direct instruction? Could they? Even if some students were able to discover that *sh* says /sh/ on their own over time, it certainly would not be an efficient way of learning. Yet, as you can see in this mini-lesson, the explicit instruction is direct, time-efficient, and effective.

Working through the gradual release of responsibility, then, we would proceed to guided instruction.

Guided Instruction: *We do*

Shared reading is an excellent example of student practice with teacher support. During a shared reading experience, the students read with me. As we read together, we are looking for the grapheme *sh* along the way. Perhaps I have asked students to put their hands on their head (or stand up and sit back down) when we come across a word with *sh*, and then they say the word with me. I can provide as much or as little scaffolding as the class seems to need. We are gradually releasing some of cognitive load onto the students.

As a class, we might also practice and apply our newfound knowledge of *sh* during shared writing (I scribe for the students as we write something together) and through word work (with students using individual whiteboards). Each of these learning opportunities will support our students while they practice this concept; I am present to provide the necessary support my students need.

Collaborative Practice: *You do together*

The reality is that our classrooms have students of diverse ability levels. Some students might need repeated explicit instruction, whereas others are ready to practice without direct teacher support. When I think of this stage of the gradual release of responsibility, then, I may choose to work with a small group of students who still need my support, while the other students are now able to practice with each other. What might this look like?

An efficient way to facilitate this is through literacy stations. Students work in groups of 2 to 4. Typically, the smaller the group, the more likely the on-task behavior. To keep the workload manageable for teachers, the idea of literacy stations can be kept quite simple. Already established groups (to save on time) work their way through a series of tasks. The tasks for all groups can be the same (unless some differentiation is required). Teachers might decide to have students begin with different tasks so they are not all doing the same thing, in the same area, at the same time.

In this example, the literacy stations would provide opportunities to practice with the phoneme /sh/.

- *Word Hunt:* students search for and record words with the grapheme *sh* around the classroom.
- *Word Sort:* students create a chart (*sh* at the beginning of a word, middle, end) and sort the words they found around the classroom into these categories.
- *Magnetic Letters:* students use magnetic letters on a whiteboard to create words with the grapheme *sh* that are listed for them.
- *Partner Reading:* students read a book together (perhaps a decodable book; these will be discussed later in the chapter), paying particular attention to words with *sh*.

The first two tasks could be completed in the students' word study notebooks. Before students begin the activities, I would help them prepare their notebook pages to maximize our instructional time. Also, to build in some accountability, students would hand in their notebooks at the end of the time in literacy stations. They know that I may check on what they've done.

Independent Practice: *You do alone*

With all of the practice that students have now had, our expectation is that when they encounter *sh* in context of what they are reading, they no longer say /s/ /h/ but instead make the sound /sh/. Decodable books (which follow a scope and sequence) would be excellent independent practice for students at this stage. Teachers could choose the decodable books that focus on *sh* to maximize student practice with their new phonetic knowledge.

After the teaching and scaffolding with *sh*, we would now expect to see the grapheme *sh* used to represent /sh/ more regularly when students are writing independently.

Even in this seemingly simple example, it becomes obvious that one explicit lesson is not enough to develop mastery. When we work through the gradual release of responsibility, we can deepen our students' understanding and ensure that they can apply what they've learned in various contexts. This is typically not accomplished in one day's time. Which leads us to the next section…

A Weekly Schedule

To support teachers with their planning, I suggest they create a weekly schedule for language arts. Since this is not something most teachers consider doing, facilitating time for teachers to create a weekly schedule is an effective use of staff meeting or collaborative time near the beginning of the year. Since planning in language arts is often daunting for teachers, looking at the samples and discussing a weekly schedule together can be both empowering and enlightening.

The weekly schedule should support the gradual release of responsibility and ensure that all strands of language arts are incorporated and given dedicated time. The specific focus—i.e., the content—will change each week. But the structure can remain the same. This not only ensures effective teaching, but it also makes planning in the language-arts classroom a little easier and more accessible. It gives teachers the structure they crave and supports their teaching simply by putting the key elements in place.

Following are sample schedules for Grades 1–2 and Grades 3–6. Keep in mind that these are simply examples. Your teachers may create something different, based on the school timetable or staffing. The point is not that the schedule should be identical to what you see here. However, the sample schedules on page 33 can provide a starting point and remind teachers of the necessary components.

On these sample schedules, you will notice a mini-lesson on Monday. You can remind teachers that the mini-lesson should ground the week and guide the discussion and practice for students throughout the week. Is it the only mini-lesson in language arts that week? Likely not. But it will be one of the main focuses for the week, often with other mini-lessons supporting it. For example, if we taught *sh* during the mini-lesson on Monday, we could follow up with another mini-lesson on the digraph *th* later in the week.

By now, you recognize that the elements within the weekly schedule are not isolated from each other. In fact, they are inseparably connected. In our example using the teaching of the digraph *sh*, you can see how all the stages within the gradual release of responsibility would fit into a weekly schedule like this one. In our example, two areas of the Grades 1 and 2 weekly timetables—phonics

Although teachers may plan and discuss their schedules collaboratively, each teacher creates their own weekly schedule for their own classroom.

For your reference, **blends** are two letters that come together but each letter maintains their individual sounds, such as *fr*, *st*, *gl*, and *sw*. **Digraphs** are two letters that come together and create a new sound, such as *sh*, *wh*, *th*, and *ph*.

Grades 1–2				
Monday	**Tuesday**	**Wednesday**	**Thursday**	**Friday**
Journal Writing Independent Reading	Independent Reading	Independent Reading	Independent Reading	Independent Reading
Morning Message	Morning Message	Morning Message	Morning Message	Morning Message
Phonemic Awareness/ Phonics	Phonemic Awareness/ Phonics	Phonemic Awareness/ Phonics	Phonemic Awareness/ Phonics	Phonemic Awareness/ Phonics
Word Study (including introducing new word-wall words)	Small-Group Instruction/ Literacy Stations	Small-Group Instruction/ Literacy Stations	Writing • targeted mini-lesson • exploration of mentor texts • modelled/shared writing • independent writing (revision)	Small-Group Instruction/ Literacy Stations
Mini-lesson Monday • read-aloud • shared reading/ writing		Reader Response (writing in response to a read-aloud or other text in some form)		Freewriting
Talk Time will be embedded throughout the week in the form of turn-and-talk opportunities, thinking routines, and collaborative learning strategies.				

Grades 3–6				
Monday	**Tuesday**	**Wednesday**	**Thursday**	**Friday**
Journal Writing Independent Reading	Independent Reading	Independent Reading	Independent Reading	Independent Reading
Word Study (including introducing new word-wall words)	Small-Group Instruction/ Literacy Stations	Word Study (word patterns, morphology, etc.)	Writing • targeted mini-lesson • exploration of mentor texts • modelled/shared writing • independent writing (revision)	Word Study (word patterns, morphology, etc.)
Mini-lesson Monday • read-aloud • shared reading/ writing	Freewriting	Reader Response (writing in response to a read-aloud or other text in some form)		Small-Group Instruction/ Literacy Stations Freewriting
Talk Time will be embedded throughout the week in the form of turn-and-talk opportunities, thinking routines, and collaborative learning strategies.				

Just as some administrators ask teachers to submit their timetables and/or year plans, you might decide to collect the teachers' weekly language-arts schedules. If you do, remind teachers that it is a way for you to learn and stay informed about classroom practice, rather than being judgmental in nature.

and the mini-lesson—overlap. This will especially be the case early in the year. Other weeks, though, we may have another focus for our Monday mini-lesson. The weekly schedule reminds us that, in Grade 1 and 2, phonemic awareness and phonics should be a part of our daily work. It should also be embedded throughout the day. In addition to the time on the schedule, teachers can reinforce the teaching of these skills quite naturally in other subject areas and even during transition times. For example, during the read-aloud for social studies, perhaps students notice the digraph *sh* and the teacher takes the time to reinforce this learning.

The Importance of Routine

When planning the weekly schedule, note that certain activities become daily routines. For example, every day begins with independent reading. In my sample, the only exception to this is Mondays. When my students come into class on Monday mornings, they find their journals (with my response to last week's entry) waiting for them on their desks. Students know their week begins with journal writing and look forward to my response from the week before. It is a routine we have established, so there is no instruction required on my part. As they finish their journals, they begin independent reading.

Another routine I embed into my weekly schedule is the addition of words to the classroom word wall. By including it in the weekly schedule, we are likely to be more consistent with this practice.

What routines do your teachers have in place?

One of the benefits of establishing strong routines is that we capitalize on instruction time and minimize transition time. In Chapter 1 we discussed school-wide practices. These school-wide practices affect our teachers' timetabling and planning. Whenever possible, then, these practices should be discussed and created collaboratively. And if we do have daily announcements or broadcast, beginning at a consistent time is key to ensuring that teachers can plan their instructional time accordingly.

> "Planning can be done in many ways, but the most powerful is when teachers work together to develop plans, develop common understandings of what is worth teaching, collaborate on understanding their beliefs of challenge and progress, and work together to evaluate the impact of their planning on student outcomes." (Hattie 2012, 37)

Resources to Support Language-Arts Instruction

Imagine this: A teacher new to Grade 2 enters their classroom for the first time. They find student resources for mathematics, science, and social studies. They search for the language-arts resources. Not finding them, they go to a colleague to ask about them. A colleague's response might be: "Did you find your classroom library?" "I have a few teacher resources you could borrow." "Do you have your own picture books?" Quite frankly, there likely will not be a response that will satisfy or calm a teacher new to the teaching of language arts in elementary school. There are certainly resources that teachers can refer to, but there is not one resource to guide the planning or instruction of the entire language-arts curriculum. There is also not one student resource that teachers will use.

If you are the administrator supporting this teacher, what do you tell them? How do you help?

Teachers are going to need resources to help them understand how to teach the various components of language arts and they are going to need resources to use with students. Whether your school purchases these for your teachers or teachers are expected to purchase them on their own, it is helpful to have some suggestions for them.

Teacher Resources

Teacher resources can be purchased for the school library so that all teachers have access to them. In my experience, though, some teachers prefer to have their own copy to refer to regularly and annotate for themselves. It is helpful if teachers have a solid resource to target the following components of language arts:

See page 129 for specific recommended resources in each of the areas outlined here. The resources are applicable, regardless of your provincial curriculum, as they will support strong pedagogy in the area of language arts.

- teaching reading
- teaching writing
- teaching phonics (K–2)
- teaching word study and vocabulary
- general instruction and best practice

Without one specific resource, you can see why it can be overwhelming to tackle the teaching of language arts, especially the first time. To support teachers with their planning and instruction of language arts, some schools decide to purchase a common book for the entire staff to help guide conversation about pedagogy and instruction: a book related to the school literacy goal, perhaps.

Mentor Texts

It is also essential that our teachers have access to a collection of mentor texts. *Mentor texts* refers to texts teachers use with students as examples of good writing and to texts they use to teach specific genres or skills. The most effective mentor texts in elementary classrooms tend to be picture books. They are used to study the author's craft and often provide the basis of mini-lessons on writing.

Over time, teachers typically gather a collection of their favorite mentor texts. As a school, though, it can be helpful to purchase some of these books for the school library. In my previous teacher resources on the teaching of writing, I list many mentor texts specific to genres or skills we are teaching. I know of many schools who have used these lists to purchase mentor texts that all teachers in their school have access to. Unlike a teacher resource that teachers will likely want to use throughout the year and annotate in some way, mentor texts can easily be shared between teachers, as they are most often used for a limited time with each class. And if the expectation is that teachers use powerful literature as mentor texts, providing some of these books for teacher use is always appreciated! (More on this in Chapter 7.)

Student Resources

Students require access to resources, too! There are a few different types of resources to consider.

A Classroom Library

A strong classroom library includes many genres and types of text: fiction (picture books, chapter books, novels, graphic novels), nonfiction, magazines, poetry, etc. Student interests and abilities vary greatly and the classroom library should accommodate and engage all of our students. It should therefore include a range of topics, genres, and reading levels. It is also important to look at our classroom libraries with a lens of equity and inclusion: are all of our students represented in the books on our shelves?

Every few years, schools can look at updating and adding to classroom libraries as new books are introduced. In some provinces, parent councils might be able to purchase books for classroom libraries. Check the rules in your area.

Decodable Books

Decodable books have become more popular as many provinces return to a more intentional teaching of phonics. The power of decodable books is that students can practice their phonetic knowledge in context, rather than having phonics remain an isolated skill. Decodable books follow a scope and sequence, with new graphemes and phonemes introduced gradually. Where leveled books include many words that cannot be easily decoded and can frustrate students, decodable books help build confidence in beginning readers as they practice what they have learned. We haven't talked much about it yet but, since reading is such a complex skill, building confidence is an important aspect of teaching our students to read. Decodable books can help with our newest readers. Keep in mind that decodable books would typically be found in Grade 1 and 2 classrooms. They might also be used for intervention purposes with older students and to support English Language Learners.

An Online Library

Online libraries have been around for quite some time. During the pandemic, they became more popular, as teachers scrambled to give their students access to books. As a result, the number of online libraries increased dramatically. When considering a subscription for your classrooms, explore the options and consider these questions:

As a language-arts consultant during the pandemic, I explored many online libraries for students. Many are excellent. There were a few, though, that turned me off immediately because they were not user-friendly, easy to navigate, or visually appealing.

- Is the library diverse in genre, topic, and cultural representation?
- Is the format user-friendly and pleasing to the eye for students? Is the display customizable?
- Can students choose what they want to read?
- Can teachers assign specific books to students?
- Is there an audio option that enables students to hear the books being read to them?
- Is there an option that allows students to record themselves reading and play it back?
- Are there features that your teachers would like to see included: teaching notes, filters for finding specific topics/genres/subject areas/reading levels, assessment tools, ways of monitoring student reading, etc.?
- Are decodable books included?

Instructional Walk Considerations: Planning and Resources

After reading and thinking more about planning and resources, consider these questions on your next instructional walk:

- Do teachers work through the gradual release of responsibility by teaching explicitly; allowing for practice and reinforcement through structures, such as guided reading and literacy stations; and ensuring time for independent practice?
- Do teachers engage in the explicit teaching of skills? Are mini-lessons (on reading, writing, word study, etc.) a regular part of language-arts instruction?
- Are there routines established in your classrooms? How can you tell?
- If there are literacy stations set up within classrooms, are students meaningfully engaged? Is there a measure in place to ensure student accountability?
- If students are moving between stations, are transitions quick and efficient?
- How current and diverse are the classroom libraries within your school?
- Do teachers or students need additional resources?

Talk Time: Planning and Resources

Have a look at these sample weekly schedules and the diagram that illustrates the Gradual Release of Responsibility. Then discuss the questions with your colleagues.

Grades 1–2				
Monday	**Tuesday**	**Wednesday**	**Thursday**	**Friday**
Journal Writing Independent Reading	Independent Reading	Independent Reading	Independent Reading	Independent Reading
Morning Message	Morning Message	Morning Message	Morning Message	Morning Message
Phonemic Awareness/Phonics	Phonemic Awareness/Phonics	Phonemic Awareness/Phonics	Phonemic Awareness/Phonics	Phonemic Awareness/Phonics
Word Study (including introducing new word-wall words)	Small-Group Instruction/ Literacy Stations	Small-Group Instruction/ Literacy Stations	Writing • targeted mini-lesson • exploration of mentor texts • modelled/ shared writing • independent writing (revision)	Small-Group Instruction/ Literacy Stations
Mini-lesson Monday • read-aloud • shared reading/ writing		Reader Response (writing in response to a read-aloud or other text in some form)		Freewriting
Talk Time will be embedded throughout the week in the form of turn-and-talk opportunities, thinking routines, and collaborative learning strategies.				

Grades 3–6				
Monday	**Tuesday**	**Wednesday**	**Thursday**	**Friday**
Journal Writing Independent Reading	Independent Reading	Independent Reading	Independent Reading	Independent Reading
Word Study (including introducing new word-wall words)	Small-Group Instruction/ Literacy Stations	Word Study (word patterns, morphology, etc.)	Writing • targeted mini-lesson • exploration of mentor texts • modelled/ shared writing • independent writing (revision)	Word Study (word patterns, morphology, etc.)
Mini-lesson Monday • read-aloud • shared reading/ writing	Freewriting	Reader Response (writing in response to a read-aloud or other text in some form)		Small-Group Instruction/ Literacy Stations Freewriting
Talk Time will be embedded throughout the week in the form of turn-and-talk opportunities, thinking routines, and collaborative learning strategies.				

Pembroke Publishers ©2023 *Literacy Leadership Matters* by Karen Filewych ISBN 978-1-55138-361-3

Talk Time: Planning and Resources (cont'd)

I Do	We Do	You Do It Together	You Do It Alone
Explicit Instruction	Guided Instruction	Collaborative Practice (without teacher guidance)	Independent Practice
teacher as **model**	teacher as **guide**	teacher as **resource**	teacher as **observer**

Gradual Release of Responsibility →

- What do you think of the idea of a weekly language-arts schedule? Is it something you already have in place? Use these examples to create (or tweak) a weekly language-arts schedule.
- Consider how you will embed the essential components and routines into your schedule.
- What does a mini-lesson look like in your classroom? How often do you engage in mini-lessons with your class?
- Do you have time scheduled during the week to support each stage of the gradual release of responsibility: explicit instruction, guided instruction, collaborative practice, independent practice?
- How do you ensure accountability during small-group work or literacy stations?

Resources

- Which teacher resources do you find most helpful in language arts? Why?
- Is there an area within language arts in which you would like more support?
- Consider your classroom library. Do your students have access to books of different genres, topics, and levels? Do you notice any gaps in your classroom library?

4

Oral Language

"Reading and writing float on a sea of talk."
— James Britton

If you were to ask the parents of your students this question—"What is the most important skill you want your child to learn in elementary school?"—what do you think they'd say? I predict most would say reading. Reading is the key that unlocks the doors of knowledge and opportunity, that enables us to function in the world.

In this chapter, yet again, we are going to see how much the strands of language interact and support one another in language learning. The focus on oral language—listening and speaking—supports our students' reading in significant (and sometimes unexpected) ways. In fact, an intentional focus on oral language in our classrooms may help prevent some of the reading difficulties certain students encounter.

In 1986, Philip Gough and William Tunmer proposed the **Simple View of Reading**. They presented their theory as a mathematical equation:

Word Recognition × Language Comprehension = Reading Comprehension

Understanding the theories of learning to read is helpful when you are supporting teachers in reading instruction and justifying decisions to parents. This understanding could also help you determine what type of intervention might be necessary for students.

The crux of their theory is that both word recognition and language comprehension are necessary for skilled reading. *Word recognition* refers to decoding or word reading; *language comprehension* refers to the ability to understand the elements of language, such as vocabulary, background knowledge, and language structures. Language comprehension is sometimes referred to as listening comprehension, and children acquire these skills through exposure and practice with oral language.

In 2001, Dr. Hollis Scarborough published what is widely known as **Scarborough's Reading Rope**. She outlined the skills required for both word recognition and language comprehension, and showed how these strands are woven together in skilled readers. Within language comprehension, she includes background knowledge, vocabulary, language structures, verbal reasoning, and literacy knowledge. Within word recognition, she includes phonological awareness, decoding, and sight recognition. Scarborough's Reading Rope is an excellent visual to keep in mind when thinking about the skills required in reading.

From Scarborough, H. S. (2001). "Connecting early language and literacy to later reading (dis)abilities: Evidence, theory, and practice." In S. Neuman & D. Dickinson (Eds.), *Handbook of Early Literacy Research* (page 98). New York, NY: Guilford Press. Reprinted with permission of Guilford Press.

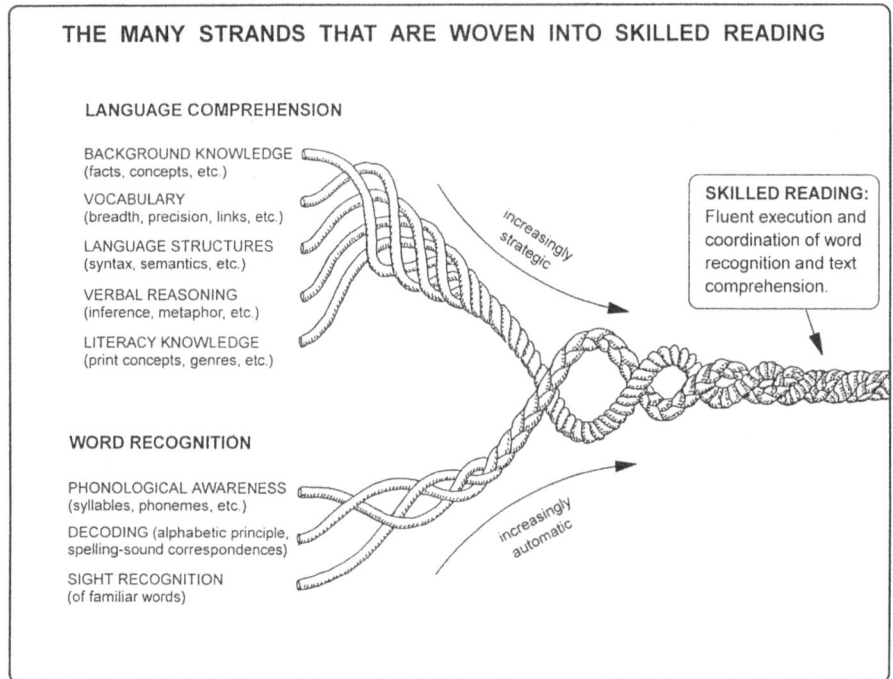

THE MANY STRANDS THAT ARE WOVEN INTO SKILLED READING

LANGUAGE COMPREHENSION

BACKGROUND KNOWLEDGE (facts, concepts, etc.)

VOCABULARY (breadth, precision, links, etc.)

LANGUAGE STRUCTURES (syntax, semantics, etc.)

VERBAL REASONING (inference, metaphor, etc.)

LITERACY KNOWLEDGE (print concepts, genres, etc.)

increasingly strategic

SKILLED READING: Fluent execution and coordination of word recognition and text comprehension.

WORD RECOGNITION

PHONOLOGICAL AWARENESS (syllables, phonemes, etc.)

DECODING (alphabetic principle, spelling-sound correspondences)

SIGHT RECOGNITION (of familiar words)

increasingly automatic

To better understand these theories, let's consider children who are skilled in one area but not the other. As we do, remember the goal of reading is reading comprehension. Why read if we cannot understand what it is we're reading?

Student A

Student A is an excellent decoder. If we were listening to her read, we might assume that she can understand the text because she pronounces the words correctly. And yet Student A does not have strong language comprehension skills (such as vocabulary, background knowledge, or language structures) so she cannot comprehend the text, even though she appears to be reading it with ease. Even if the text were read to Student A, she would still not be able to understand the meaning because of her underdeveloped language skills.

Student B

On the other hand, let's consider Student B. This child has strong language comprehension skills but he struggles to decode or read the text on his own. He would understand the passage if it were read *to* him. But without the ability to decode, he does not have access to the words on the page and therefore cannot comprehend the text.

Neither of these children are what Scarborough would call a skilled reader because neither is able to comprehend the text. As Gough and Tunmer surmised, then, we can see why both word recognition and language comprehension are necessary for reading comprehension.

These examples also demonstrate why students need different types of support to help them become stronger readers. Student A needs support with language comprehension: exposure to and practice with vocabulary, background knowledge, verbal reasoning, and the structures of language itself. Much of the content within this chapter is going to support Student A. Sometimes teachers will attempt to support Student A with a myriad of comprehension strategies. As Burkins and Yates (2021) say, "children struggling with comprehension need more than comprehension strategies. They need abundant opportunities to use and develop language and to build knowledge" (21). They go on to say,

> … in the early years, while children are learning to read … we must have an eye toward the future, focusing on stretching the limits of listening comprehension through oral language development and knowledge building. (21)

But let's not forget that Student B needs support, too. His challenge, however, is decoding. The strategies in the upcoming chapters which deal with phonological awareness and phonics are going to be necessary to support this student with his reading comprehension. Will he still benefit from the oral language work within our classroom? Absolutely. Not only can language comprehension skills always be strengthened, but we also know how the very nature of language can support all learning.

Knowing how important oral language is to reading comprehension, to learning in general, why wouldn't we ensure a strong oral language component within our classrooms? Oral language supports and develops our students' learning in many ways:

- building vocabulary and background knowledge
- contributing to the understanding of the structure and syntax of language
- improving verbal reasoning
- providing opportunities to better understand content and construct meaning

Oral language is also part of our language-arts curriculum, with its own specific outcomes. When we look at the oral language components of curricula across the country, there are many similarities, although the wording may vary:

- practicing listening and responding appropriately in various contexts
- following directions
- understanding oral language traditions
- speaking and presenting in various forms (stories, poems, reports, dramatizations)
- using and adjusting elements, such as volume, tone, pace, intonation, and phrasing, when speaking
- reading and understanding body language and facial expressions
- understanding how oral language assists with learning

At a quick glance, this list seems extensive. It is important to remember, though, that much of this list can and will be accomplished in conjunction with other outcomes in language arts and also in other subject areas.

Vygotsky once said, "By giving our students practice in talking with others, we give them frames for thinking on their own."

Do the teachers in your school place value on oral language? If so, how can you tell? If not, what might you do to change this?

The remainder of this chapter is divided into two main sections: oral language to support learning, and opportunities to practice oral language development. Still, much of the content overlaps. I may be using oral language to support learning while developing oral language in the process!

Oral Language to Support Learning

The Art of Questioning

As educators, we know that effective questioning can help students become more active and engaged in the lessons we teach. Sometimes the questions we ask are simply a check-in: a thumbs-up or thumbs-down response could be all we require. However, it is also essential that we invite students into deeper thinking and more reflective responses through carefully crafted questions: questions that focus on broader concepts, questions that require students to make connections or comparisons, questions that push our students' thinking beyond their own experiences. Bloom's Taxonomy comes to mind. In 2001, Lorin Anderson, a former student of Benjamin Bloom, revised the taxonomy, and his revisions have become widely accepted.

Bloom's Taxonomy categorizes thinking skills. It is important that our students are able to remember and understand ideas (considered the lower-order thinking skills), but we want to push our students to higher levels, as well (applying, analyzing, evaluating, and creating). Questioning of all types should occur in all areas of the curriculum.

Revised version of Bloom's Taxonomy

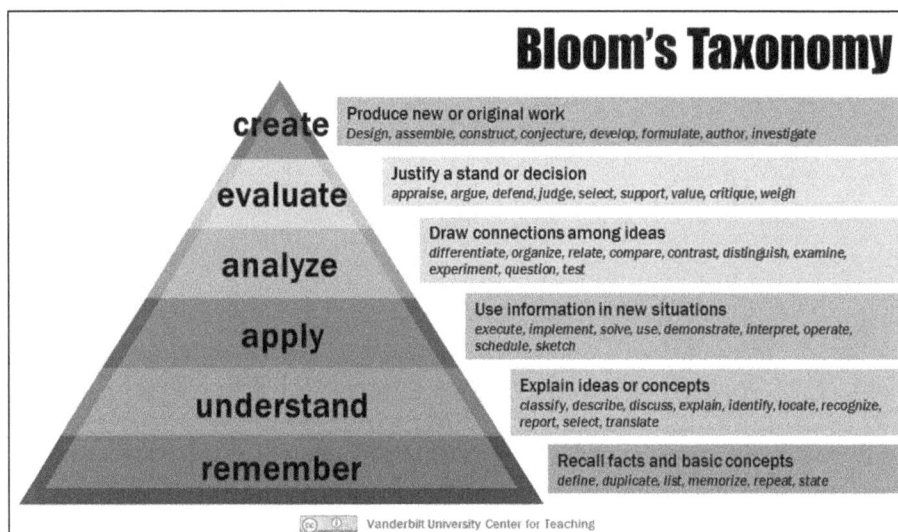

Bloom's Taxonomy

create
Produce new or original work
Design, assemble, construct, conjecture, develop, formulate, author, investigate

evaluate
Justify a stand or decision
appraise, argue, defend, judge, select, support, value, critique, weigh

analyze
Draw connections among ideas
differentiate, organize, relate, compare, contrast, distinguish, examine, experiment, question, test

apply
Use information in new situations
execute, implement, solve, use, demonstrate, interpret, operate, schedule, sketch

understand
Explain ideas or concepts
classify, describe, discuss, explain, identify, locate, recognize, report, select, translate

remember
Recall facts and basic concepts
define, duplicate, list, memorize, repeat, state

Vanderbilt University Center for Teaching

Questions in the *remember* and *understand* levels of Bloom's Taxonomy typically expect "right" answers: they call for basic recall or explanations. Although there is a place for this, it is also important to consider asking students more open-ended questions. Bright (2021) explains how she intentionally asks students an open-ended question:

> After reading a story or an excerpt from a story, my favourite question to ask students is, "What did you think of that?" (24).

On your next instruction walk, pay close attention to the types of questions teachers are asking their students. Also consider what types of questions you tend to use during interactions with your teachers. Are the questions open-ended? Do they invite varied responses?

I can imagine the varied responses she would hear! Some students might comment on the content, some on how they feel, others on the tone or mood of the writing, still others on the style or techniques used by the author. The open-ended question values and invites all responses. It also exposes students to different ways of thinking.

In *Disrupting Thinking*, Kyleen Beers and Robert Probst (2017) describe the different types of questions as monologic and dialogic:

> By monologic, we mean the sorts of questions to which there is a right, or best, answer. They can be useful in checking to see whether or not the students were actually paying attention.… Dialogic questions, on the other hand, are questions that may not have quick and easy answers, but are usually much more discussable. (152)

It is through dialogic questions that students engage in meaningful conversation with their peers when they have an opportunity to think aloud and express their points of view. Fisher, Frey, and Hattie (2017) remind us, "An important role of the teacher is to foster questions and dialogue among students and create meaningful experiences that allow them to interact with one another" (13). As we discussed in Chapter 2, all students should have the opportunity to formulate answers and articulate their thinking. Ensuring there are structures in place for this (turn-and-talk, cooperative learning structures, etc.) within our classrooms is essential. Our English Language Learners will benefit from these processes, but so will all our students.

As administrators, we should also strive to create this same experience for our teachers. Teachers will feel heard and valued, and will be much more willing to collaborate, in an environment where questions and dialogue are encouraged.

As important as it is for educators to ask effective questions of their students, it is just as important for students to learn how to ask good questions. This does not always come naturally to students, but is an important skill for them to practice. It can assist them in their own learning in all areas of the curriculum.

Teachers might not be familiar with this strategy. Or they may never have considered its value. At an upcoming staff meeting where you discuss the benefits of oral language, choose an image to share with your staff to demonstrate and discuss this strategy and its benefits.

An effective way to improve the quality and diversity of questions is through the use of visuals. After showing students an interesting image (photograph, painting, or advertisement), we can ask questions of our students and encourage them to do the same. The resulting discussion exposes students to diverse vocabulary, helps them practice the structure and syntax of language, and builds background knowledge in the process. To help students new to the language feel more comfortable sharing their questions, teachers might divide the class into smaller groups and give each group an image about which they ask and record questions. The images could then be rotated from group to group. Perhaps one image is a close-up picture of an insect on a leaf. Another might be of a group of protesters or two children in tears sitting on the front steps of a home. Yet another could show a farmyard with destruction caused by a storm. Each of these images would require different vocabulary, lead to different questions, and require students to rely on (and build) their background knowledge.

The Art of Listening

Is listening a skill we need to teach? Do our students know how to listen?

I don't know about you, but I'm not always a good listener. Sometimes I become distracted when someone is talking, and—too often—I begin to formulate my response before I've even had a chance to hear everything being said. In fact, I have to be quite intentional to ensure I am listening well. The act of listening might seem a passive experience, and yet the term *active listening* has become quite common. There are times that passive listening is acceptable: if I have music playing softly while I work, for example. Yet most often listening requires much more active attention. When I make a concerted effort to stop what I am doing and make eye contact with the individual speaking, I am much more likely to pay attention to their words. Even then, though, I use strategies to keep me focused.

When you walk around your school, can you tell if your students are listening? Really listening? It's hard to know. After all, listening is an internal behavior that others cannot see. As a teacher, I've been caught a few times when I assumed a student wasn't listening because of what I saw—doodling or constant foot tapping, for example—and then was surprised when those students were not only able to provide an on-topic answer, but an insightful one! Looks can be deceiving.

Consider the role of listening in our classrooms. Who are our students listening to? For what purpose? The answers to those questions are going to vary throughout the day. Just as we want our students to be aware of how they use language, we also want them to be aware of *how* and *why* they're listening, *when* they listen best, and *what helps* them listen.

Back to the question then: Is listening a skill we have to teach? I'd say so. It's part of understanding ourselves as learners. How do I listen best? What helps me to listen? What distracts me? When our students know that these answers are not the same for everyone, they begin to recognize their own tendencies and understand that they might listen and learn differently from their peers.

Oral Language as Scaffolding

Before my students and I write, we often talk. This talk is intentional. Think of writing from a student's point of view. If I have given my students something to write about, there are two significant tasks inherent in this assignment: 1) develop content and 2) communicate that content through writing. If we consider how new the skill of writing is to our students (not to mention how difficult), this can be especially daunting. Not only do they have to decide *what* to write but they also have to figure out *how* to write it. Talking about a topic first helps students generate ideas. By the time they actually pick up the pencil to write, they have some idea of where to begin and what they want to say. This allows the second task to become the focus: the act of **encoding**, deciding which letters form which words, putting words together to form sentences.

Oral language is not only a scaffold before writing. It can be used to support our students' thinking and learning in many circumstances throughout the day.

Oral Language as Differentiation

If you notice teachers reading tests to students or scribing an individual student's answers, recognize this as differentiation, supporting students on their learning journeys.

Have you ever taught a student you know is full of knowledge and information but does poorly on written exams? Was it the reading (decoding or comprehension) of the questions that posed the problem? Was it formulating a written answer that proved difficult? Perhaps both. Because reading and writing are such complex tasks, students who are still emerging in these areas might have difficulty with traditional forms of assessment. As language teachers, we will continue to support students with the skills of reading and writing. But we also have to recognize that sometimes our assessment methods are biased. Some students will flourish if an exam is read to them or if they can answer orally instead of in written form. In each circumstance, we should be aware of what we are trying to assess. If the answer is, for example, concepts and knowledge in science, then we must not let a student's difficulty with reading and writing get in the way of communicating what they know.

In her 2007 book *Proust and the Squid*, Maryanne Wolf, a cognitive neuro-scientist and child development expert, says,

> We were never born to read. Human beings invented reading only a few thousand years ago. And with this invention, we rearranged the very organization of our brain, which in turn expanded the ways we were able to think, which altered the intellectual evolution of our species. Reading is one of the single most remarkable inventions in history… (3)

Remarkable, yes, and extremely complex. For this reason, oral language might be necessary as differentiation for some of our students.

Opportunities to Practice Oral Language Skills

Presentations

Within our provincial language-arts curricula across the country, there are outcomes related to presentation skills. The ability to speak in front of our peers—informally and formally—is a necessary skill, one that brings with it varying levels of comfort. Presentations can begin with our youngest students, but at that point should remain informal. I've mentioned low-stakes writing; the same premise should be considered with presentations. There should be many opportunities to practice presenting to a group of peers or to the class without assessment. For many students, presenting is stressful enough; knowing that they are being evaluated on the presentation raises the stakes considerably. Book talks are a fantastic way to ease into presenting to peers. How might you encourage or facilitate book talks in other classrooms within the school?

I encourage Five-Finger Book Talks. The presentation is kept simple but still encourages students to speak in front of their peers.

1. Title
2. Author
3. Genre
4. Brief Summary
5. Recommendation

Choral Reading

When I was a beginning teacher, I found myself in a school where choral reading was common. It was so common, in fact, that many classes were entered into a festival to perform and compete against other schools. While I don't see a need for festival performances, the process involved in choral reading can be powerful for students. It is a safe way to practice many of the skills referred to in our curriculum for oral language.

What is choral reading? Choral reading refers to the reading aloud of text together by a whole class or a group of students. Often, teachers use poetry for choral reading. The process can help build fluency, improve student confidence (especially for those who struggle with reading independently or who are nervous reading in front of others), and provide opportunities for teachers to discuss and improve such qualities as volume, tone, pace, intonation, and phrasing during reading. We can draw our students' attention to punctuation, too. The time we spend on one piece of text can also help to improve comprehension and, as a result, expression.

Shel Silverstein and Dennis Lee poems are wonderful for choral reading. They lend themselves to expression and joyful reading! Two of my favorites by Shel Silverstein: *Sarah Cynthia Sylvia Stout Would Not Take the Garbage Out* and *Sick*. Students will be engaged and perhaps even motivated to read more poetry.

Does your school have Holiday concerts, Spring concerts, or other performance-based events? Do you have a music teacher to support the preparation for these events or does preparation fall on your classroom teachers? Choral reading can be a way for teachers to prepare something for a concert (if that is the expectation) and accomplish curricular objectives in the process.

Typically, I begin by reading the poem to my students. Then, I show students the text and we read through it once or twice together. After I explain what we are going to do with the poem, we discuss how we might divide the poem into different parts. We talk and debate about which lines will be read by us all together, which lines could be read by a smaller group of students, and which lines could be read by one student for emphasis.

Consider the oral language at work during a discussion such as this! Students are proposing an idea and justifying why they think text should be read in a particular way. Other students are listening and responding. Students tend to become quite passionate about their ideas and invested in the process.

Eventually, we have marked up the text, indicating who will read what. Then, repeated readings begin until we are fluent and expressive. Just as we had conversations about who will read what, we can also talk about how and where we can add more expression or change the volume, pace, and phrasing to get the meaning across to the listener. Students love this process! I love it, too, because not only am I addressing many of my language-arts outcomes, but I am also watching my students playfully engage with language.

Obviously, this process cannot occur within one day. It is something we return to repeatedly for a few days. And although I don't see the need for a festival, performing for another class or the school can be motivation for practice, which leads to many readings of the poem.

Debate

Ask your teachers to invite you into their classroom during a debate. You will learn a lot about the students in your school!

The word *debate* has negative connotations for some. However, bringing debate into our classrooms can be a powerful tool to improve language development and hone language skills, while reinforcing content curriculum. Often, I engage students in debate on a topic in social studies or science. Again, there is no need for formality (although students may push for more formality, especially in the older grades). All that is required is an engaging topic—for example, *Should zoos be banned?*—and some time.

Once the topic is decided, I put all of the students arguing *for* on one side of the room and all of the students arguing *against* on the other side. I give them time to develop arguments together. Even before the debate begins, students are using diverse language skills, such as listening to their peers, jotting notes, forming arguments, justifying their reasons, and anticipating counter arguments. I remind them how language is at work during this process to make them more aware of why we are doing what we are doing. And don't be fooled into thinking that debate is effective only with older students; I have witnessed many lively debates by students as young as Grade 1. Topics that stimulate lively debate are often related to the environment or issues that directly affect students' lives in some way: school uniforms, homework, the abolishment of recess, etc.

Honoring Language Traditions

Many of our Canadian classrooms have become much more diverse. The language traditions of the cultures represented can also be quite diverse. Culture, stories, and traditions are often shared through oral communication, especially from one generation to another. This concept is now included in many provincial curricula.

Students are often not aware of their family's or culture's language traditions. Teachers might decide to use this topic as a way of improving their students' language skills, having them interview a parent or grandparent. Consider the many skills involved in this process:

- developing relevant and appropriate questions to ask a family member
- interviewing a family member
- recording the information shared by this person
- organizing the gathered ideas
- sharing the ideas with their peers

An assignment such as this uses language skills while honoring the language traditions of the families within your school. Why not consider this topic on a school-wide level?

Honor the Diversity Within Your School Community

Choose a central bulletin board and begin by posting a map of the world. Add photos and text to highlight where families are from and what language(s) they speak. What a wonderful way to pay tribute to your families and their diverse backgrounds! Who could create this bulletin board? Perhaps a class who has developed a survey during math class. After gathering data, they could post their results. Or perhaps you decide to create a committee of parents to volunteer in your school. This would be a meaningful way to include newcomer families, involve them in school life, provide them with a way to practice their English, and allow them to meet other parents in the community. A worthwhile endeavor indeed!

Instructional Walk Considerations: Oral Language

After reading and thinking more about the indispensable nature of oral language, consider these questions on your next instructional walk:

- How are teachers building vocabulary and background knowledge with their students?
- Do you hear teachers asking their students various types of questions?
- Do the questions require more than a yes or no answer? Are they sometimes open-ended? Do they require students to use higher-order thinking skills?
- Do students have ample time to think about and answer the questions?
- Do teachers use oral language to support their students' learning as scaffolding (talk before writing, for example) and as differentiation (e.g., reading test questions to students)?
- Do students have diverse opportunities to practice their oral language skills: presentations, choral reading, and debate?

Talk Time: Oral Language

Take some time to read and think about this quotation and these questions before discussing them with your colleagues.

In their book *Shifting the Balance*, Burkins and Yates (2021) remind us,

> … if children cannot understand enough of the words and sentences when they are spoken, they will not comprehend the same words and sentences when they read them. This means that opportunities to grow oral language—including vocabulary, background knowledge, sentence structure, and more—actually develop the comprehension mechanisms of reading." (17)

- How do you bring oral language—listening and speaking—into your classroom? In what subject areas? In what contexts?
- How do you build vocabulary and background knowledge with your students?
- What makes a good question? Are you deliberate in asking a variety of question types with your students?
- Do you push your students' thinking further by asking for clarification or more detail: "What makes you think that?" or "Can anyone explain _____'s answer in another way?"
- Do your students have opportunities to practice their oral language skills through presentations, choral reading, and debate?

Pembroke Publishers ©2023 *Literacy Leadership Matters* by Karen Filewych ISBN 978-1-55138-361-3

5

Word Study

"Respect the building blocks, master the fundamentals, and the
potential is unlimited."
— PJ Ladd

The content of this chapter may be what you, as an administrator, find yourself answering questions about more and more frequently, questions posed by
teachers and parents. With all the media attention now given to phonological
awareness and the so-called return to phonics, it can be helpful to understand
the background and research behind the resurgence of these foundational skills.

In the preceding chapter, we discussed the Simple View of Reading by Gough
and Tunmer, in which one of the skills necessary for reading comprehension is
word recognition. After all, how can we read if we cannot recognize the words
on the page? Scarborough's Reading Rope also highlights the importance of word
recognition, breaking it into these sections: **phonological awareness**, decoding,
and sight recognition. In *Beginning to Read*, Marilyn Adams (1994) says,

> Only if your ability to recognize and capture the meaning of the words on a page
> is rapid, effortless, and automatic will you have available the cognitive energy and
> resources upon which skillful comprehension depends. (5)

Evidently, word recognition is essential. Why word study, then? Word study
ensures our students have the ability and capacity to read words rapidly, effort-
lessly, and automatically. If word recognition is our goal, word study is the process through which we meet that goal.

Have you ever wondered how many words there are in the English language?
The possible combinations of letters form hundreds of thousands of words; some
suggest more than a million. Teachers certainly can't teach their students each and
every word. Word study focuses on understanding the patterns in words; knowing the patterns enables students to learn many words that follow those patterns.
But even before this is possible, our students need a more basic understanding
of the parts of words: letters and their corresponding sounds. In order to read,
in order to reach our ultimate goal of reading comprehension, our students must
first learn these foundations. Understanding the fundamentals will empower

students as readers and help develop a positive relationship between themselves and text.

I have sometimes heard presumptions about the primary grades, assumptions that, because the content is "simple," so is the teaching. And yet when I taught these grade levels, I was exhausted at the end of every day. The teaching was rewarding, yes, but also demanding and complex. I always appreciated when an administrator recognized the challenges. Teaching students the complex skills of reading and writing is not an easy feat!

Understanding the Alphabetic Principle

Unless you have studied the teaching of reading, in this chapter you will likely find some vocabulary you haven't encountered before. I explain it in context but, for easy reference, the words are also included in the glossary. There may be teachers in your school who are unfamiliar with some of this vocabulary, too!

Imagine trying to learn to read without knowing the letters or the sounds they make. Letters are the building blocks for written language. In English, there are 26 letters of the alphabet. These 26 letters (either individually or in combination) make 44 sounds. The understanding that there are predictable relationships between written letters and spoken sounds is known as the **alphabetic principle**.

Unless you've been a teacher of beginning reading, perhaps there is an assumption that the alphabetic principle is simple. Maryanne Wolf's (2007) words remind us otherwise:

> At its root the alphabetic principle represents the profound insight that each word in spoken language consists of a finite group of individual sounds that can be represented by a finite group of individual letters. This seemingly innocent-sounding principle was totally revolutionary when it emerged over time, for it created the capacity for every spoken word in every language to be translated into writing. (18)

We don't often think of the origins or complexity of this system when we expect our Kindergarten and Grade 1 teachers to teach students to recognize letters, learn the corresponding sounds, and begin to use their alphabetic knowledge to read and write. But perhaps we should recognize the significance of what we are asking our students to do:

> … although it took our species roughly 2,000 years to make the cognitive breakthroughs necessary to learn to read with an alphabet, today our children have to reach those same insights about print in roughly 2,000 days. (Wolf, 2007, 19)

Whenever I read these words, the complexity of reading and writing is put into perspective. And when we recognize the complexity of teaching these skills to our students, it's no wonder there are decades-long debates about which methods are best.

Teachers often purchase these nameplates for their students using their personal funds. If the school purchased nameplates for all Grade 1 and 2 students, recognizing them for the instructional tool they are, this simple gesture would demonstrate the value placed on literacy within the school.

To support students with these foundational skills, I recommend that all Grades 1 and 2 students have an alphabet on their desks or tables for easy reference. Nameplates can be purchased that include both the upper- and lower-case alphabet above the spot for the student's name. Students will refer to this alphabet throughout the day, as they use their phonemic knowledge while writing and to remind them of proper letter formation. Although it seems such a rudimentary support for students, it is critical. I have been in primary classrooms where students do not have access to an alphabet on their desks. They have no easy access to something they should be referring to continually at this stage. We are doing these students a disservice by making the already-challenging task of letter recognition and formation even more challenging. Being able to look up to the alphabet on the wall is not enough. By the time students look back to their paper to print the letter, they may have forgotten what the letter looks like.

The Reading Wars

Mark Seidenberg (2017) suggests, "Anxiety about reading achievement underlies endless debates about how reading should be taught." (7)

You may have heard of the Reading Wars surrounding the best methods to teach reading. The pendulum swings between an explicit focus on phonics and whole language, and back and forth again, often one at the exclusion of the other. Where phonics instruction is a method of teaching reading that focuses on the alphabetic principle, whole language is a method of teaching reading that emphasizes learning whole words in meaningful contexts rather than with a focus on phonics.

When *balanced literacy* was introduced in the 1990s, some argued that the pendulum this time stopped somewhere in the middle, valuing both explicit phonics instruction and whole language. One significant change that came along with balanced literacy was the introduction of levelled texts and reading assessments, including DRA and Benchmark Assessments. Within balanced literacy, students were also taught a cueing system known as MSV. Students were encouraged to read unfamiliar text by thinking about Meaning cues (pictures, background knowledge, context clues), Syntax cues (language rules and patterns), and Visual cues (using the letters and their corresponding sounds). Balanced literacy was the go-to practice when I was a beginning teacher, and most educators teaching today have been using some form of balanced literacy, with varied levels of success.

If we are to engage in meaningful conversations about reading instruction with our teachers, we must honor their efforts and be careful not to criticize what they are currently doing. Likely, they are doing what they know and what they were taught. Engaging in learning, reflection, and discussion about their practice will yield better results than telling them to change their practice.

More recently, the **Science of Reading** (SoR) has become the latest buzz. What is the Science of Reading? The SoR refers to an extensive body of research (from the last twenty years) about how our brains learn to read. It includes scientific knowledge from experts in many disciplines, such as education, literacy, educational psychology, developmental psychology, and neurology. From this research, information has been gathered and shared about best practices for teaching reading. In his book *Reading in the Brain: The New Science of How We Read*, Stanislas Dehaene (2010) explains:

> We now know that the whole-language approach is inefficient: all children regardless of their socioeconomic backgrounds benefit from explicit and early teaching of the correspondence between letters and speech sounds. This is a well-established fact, corroborated by a great many classroom experiments. Furthermore, it is coherent with our present understanding of how the reader's brain works. (326-327)

If we understand that phonemic awareness and the explicit, systematic teaching of phonics are essential, it is important that we find out how our teachers are currently teaching phonemic awareness and phonics in our classrooms. This is where staff meeting conversations and our instructional walks become critical, all in an environment of trust.

Over the last few years, the information gleaned during this extensive research has started making its way into classrooms and new curriculum across the country. As you can see from the quote above, the research demonstrates that phonics instruction is essential. What's important to realize is that much of what we were trained to do during balanced literacy was effective and can continue. The Science of Reading is helping us put the emphasis where it belongs with our youngest readers: on phonemic awareness and the systematic, explicit teaching of phonics as prevention. The research on this is clear. Yet it's not the only data to pay attention to. The Science of Reading identifies five components that require explicit instruction: phonemic awareness, phonics, fluency, vocabulary, and comprehension. In this chapter we are going to focus on the components that fall within word study: phonemic awareness, phonics, and vocabulary. Fluency and comprehension will be discussed in Chapter 6.

Phonological Awareness, Phonemic Awareness, and Phonics: Oh My!

In *Equipped for Reading Success*, David Kilpatrick (2016) says,

> The findings from countless research studies have been consistent and clear: Students with good phonological awareness are in a great position to become good readers, while students with poor phonological awareness almost always struggle in reading. (13)

If our goal as administrators is to lead a school where students flourish, this quote should direct us. But before going further, let's be sure we have a firm understanding of the terms being used and how they differ from each other. Remember, not all teachers have a firm understanding of these terms. Understanding them yourself will help you support teachers on their learning journeys, too.

Phonological Awareness

Onset refers to the initial sound of a word (/d/ in *dog* and /tw/ in *twin*). *Rime* refers to the string of letters that follow (/og/ in *dog* and /in/ in *twin*).

Phonological awareness refers to an awareness of the sound structure of words. It is an umbrella term that includes such subsets as phonemic awareness, syllables, onset, and rime. Phonological awareness focuses solely on sounds—sounds larger than individual phonemes, such as syllables—and not yet on print. Kindergarten teachers spend much time working with their students on phonological awareness. You might see it in action when students are identifying and producing rhyming words or clapping the syllables in a word (or the words in a sentence). Teaching students to have phonological awareness involves considerable time playing with oral language!

Phonemic Awareness

Phonemes are the smallest unit of sound within a word. For example, there are three phonemes in fish: /f/ /i/ /sh/. Graphemes, on the other hand, are the written representation (a letter or combination of letters) of one sound. There are also three graphemes in fish: *f, i, sh*.

As indicated above, phonemic awareness is one subset of phonological awareness. It refers to the awareness that words are made up of distinct sounds (phonemes). You might see phonemic awareness in action when teachers are breaking a word apart (**segmenting**): dad = /d/ /a/ /d/ or **blending** a word together: /d/ /i/ /g/ = dig. Students could also be encouraged to use a mirror to notice what their mouth, lips, and tongue are doing as they produce a specific sound or phoneme: these are known as **articulatory gestures**.

Phonemic awareness is thought to be a good predictor of future literacy abilities. In her book *Speech to Print*, Louisa Cook Moats (2020) explains,

> … one of the most robust findings of modern reading research is that proficient reading and spelling are strongly associated with the ability to identify, remember, separate, combine, and manipulate phonemes, and to do so rapidly and without effort. (26)

In my own extensive work with struggling readers, it was evident that these students did not have a solid understanding of phonemes and of skills such as rhyming, segmenting words into phonemes, blending phonemes into words, and manipulating phonemes. The research shows that intentional time spent on phonemic awareness with emergent readers helps to prevent some of the reading challenges we encounter in our classrooms as students progress through the grade levels. As a principal, then, when you invest in the primary grades (specifically to support students with these foundational skills), you are acknowledging the importance of this research and working towards prevention of future reading challenges.

Phonics

"Teachers who know more about the written code of English are more favorably inclined to teach phonics and spelling to students." (Moats 2020, xxii)

Phonics is the knowledge that sounds (phonemes) are represented by letters or letter combinations (graphemes). It is with phonics that we move from a focus solely on sound and now attach those sounds to print.

There are certainly mixed reactions—by school leaders, teachers, and even parents—about the so-called *return to phonics*. Some educators never left it behind; others are hesitant to shift their focus more towards phonics. In his article "Drawing on Reading Science without Starting a War," Benjamin Riley (2020) explains his theory about the reactions of educators:

> Indeed, it's worth ruminating briefly on why many educators resist teaching phonics explicitly. My hunch is that many educators have been asked to teach phonics "explicitly" without learning the empirically supported theories that explain why phonological awareness is essential to developing literacy. What's more, teaching is an applied science; understanding the science of reading does not in and of itself lead to effective pedagogy. I strongly suspect that some teachers are hostile to phonics because phonics-based instruction, when done poorly, can be mind-numbing for students to sit through. Teachers who've seen this happen are (rightfully) concerned.

I take Benjamin Riley's theory as a cautionary tale for administrators. Our approach to adjusting instructional practices within our classrooms is critical. If teachers are told what to do without understanding why or how, they might resist or refuse changes in practice.

I was taught phonics in elementary school. And yes, I am a proficient reader and writer. However, here's what I remember about phonics instruction when I was a student: worksheets. Pages and pages of pictures with graphemes underneath to circle: *ch* or *sh*. Could memories such as these account for the concerns held by some educators? Perhaps. So, although we move back (or continue) to teach phonics, research can help understand how best to teach phonics. Forget the worksheets. Focus on consistent, explicit instruction. Give students opportunities to practice their phonetic knowledge throughout the day, through opportunities such as shared reading, reading decodable texts, and writing meaningful text. Let's explore the implications for instruction further.

What the Research Tells Us About Instruction

There is some debate—Are you surprised?—about whether phonemic awareness and phonics should be taught separately or together. There is also debate about which is more important. The research indicates there is no need to separate them and that both are essential. As Burkins and Yates (2021) emphasize,

> … learning the letters and sounds alone is clearly insufficient for success in learning to read! Helping students discover (alphabetic insight) and deepen their understanding of the alphabetic principle, therefore, requires thoughtful emphasis on phonics

and phonemic awareness—and their relationship—as two parallel and reciprocal sides of the beginning reading coin. (41)

Consider a student who knows the letter names and their corresponding sounds. Fantastic! But what we really want this student to be able to do is apply that knowledge in their reading (phonetic decoding) and writing (encoding). Applying this knowledge occurs with phonemic awareness. If students think that a word is its own unit, rather than smaller sounds coming together (most do at first), phonics will not make sense to them.

Since this book is directed to you, as administrator, it is not intended to be a comprehensive how-to guide. That being said, there are a few important takeaways from the research that can help you understand and support your teachers:

- The teaching of both phonemic awareness and phonics should be intentional and systematic.
- Teachers might need training and support in this area.
- Students benefit from noticing what their mouth, lips, and tongue are doing as they produce a specific sound or phoneme (articulatory gestures). (If your primary teachers ask for small mirrors, this is likely why!)
- Such skills as blending, segmentation, isolation, deletion, and substitution should be practiced regularly to strengthen phonemic awareness.
- Phonics instruction should follow a scope and sequence that moves from simple to complex.
- Multisensory scaffolds assist with the learning of these skills: magnetic letters, counters for Elkonin boxes, letter tiles. Teachers should have easy access to these learning tools. Although sharing between classes may save costs, these tools are used so regularly that each primary class should have their own.
- Phonemic awareness and phonics instruction should occur throughout the day, not only as one explicit daily lesson. It can be reinforced during morning messages, read-alouds, writing tasks, and transition times, and in other subject areas.
- Phonemic awareness and phonics should be taught cumulatively, regularly revisiting the learning from previous days and weeks.

Decodable Texts

Remember those decodable books that we talked about in Chapter 3? This is when they become powerful resources in our classrooms! Teachers follow a specific scope and sequence during phonics instruction. The decodable books provide students with an opportunity to practice their phonetic decoding skills in context, based on the new phonemes and graphemes that have been introduced. The Science of Reading suggests that decodable texts support our emergent readers with the skills they are being taught, which prevents future problems with reading and reduces the need for intervention with older students.

Sound Walls

You might already be familiar with word walls. With more emphasis being placed on phonemic awareness and phonics, sound walls have become increasingly popular. Sound walls display the various phonemes as they are taught. For increased effectiveness, the sounds are displayed in categories, reinforced with articulatory gestures, and referred to regularly. Sound walls are most effective in our Grade 1 and 2 classrooms. If teachers in your school are interested in creating sound

Elkonin boxes are an instructional tool used to help children improve their phonemic awareness by segmenting words into individual phonemes. In the example shown here, the child listens to and repeats the word *cat* and adds a counter to each box, representing each sound: /c/ /a/ /t/.

walls, know that they will likely require professional development to learn how to implement them effectively.

Moving to Morphology

The explicit teaching of phonemic awareness and phonics will occur primarily in our Kindergarten, Grade 1, and Grade 2 classrooms. Teachers in the older grades should continue to reinforce these concepts as needed, with the whole class and as differentiation for individual students. As well, literacy support teachers within your school should also have the knowledge and ability to support struggling readers and English Language Learners with phonemic awareness and phonics. However, word study does not end here. Once our students have a firm grasp of phonics, we begin our move to morphology.

Morphology is the study of words, how they are formed, and how they relate to other words. Specifically, we study **morphemes**. A morpheme is the smallest unit of meaning within a word. In elementary, we teach our students *prefixes, suffixes, bases*, and *roots* (often with Greek or Latin origins). Morphology can help our students decode unfamiliar words while reading, comprehend text (understanding the vocabulary and text as a whole), and ultimately improve their encoding skills (spelling and writing).

The power of morphology is evident even within this chapter. Although there may be words you are unfamiliar with, there are likely some clues within those words to help determine the meaning. Consider the words *phoneme* and *grapheme*, for example. The Greek root *phon* means "sound," whereas *graph* means "writing" in Greek. The definitions of the words reveal the connections to these morphemes: phonemes refer to a speech sound and graphemes refer to the written representation of the sound. Morphemes, then, can help us distinguish the words from one another and also understand their meaning.

Knowing the meaning of the morpheme *phon* can also help us learn and provide clues to the meaning of other words: *phonological, phonemic, microphone, megaphone, telephone, saxophone, symphony, cacophony*, etc. Knowing the meaning of the morpheme *graph* may also help with other words: *paragraph, biography, telegraph, autograph, calligraphy*, etc.

Students are often quite surprised (and empowered) when they learn that morphemes hold meaning. For example, when students learn that the prefix *re*- holds meaning (*again*), this helps them decipher the meaning of many words: *redo, rewrite, rerun, return, reread, resell, rebuild, rearrange!*

Sight Words and High-Frequency Words: One and the Same?

If our goal is word recognition, an essential component of word study involves **sight words** and **high-frequency words**. On many occasions I have heard teachers use these terms interchangeably. It can certainly be confusing! But there are important differences between the two. If you are going to engage in discussion with your teachers, it is helpful to be clear of the differences.

Sight Words

Sight words are words that are instantly recalled from memory, regardless of whether they are phonically regular or irregular. Some sight words might also be high-frequency words (*the, of, have*), but not all sight words are high-frequency words. For example, one child's **sight-word vocabulary** could include the names of their siblings (Amaya, Diego) and their favorite things (dinosaurs, ice cream). You wouldn't find these words on any high-frequency word list, but this child knows them by sight, making them, by definition, sight words.

As skilled readers, most of the words we encounter while reading have become part of our sight-word vocabulary. It is only when we encounter new terminology, such as a medical term or an animal species, that we might have to stop to decode the word. As adults, this occurs much less frequently than it does for children.

High-Frequency Words

High-frequency words are those most commonly used in the English language. They, too, can be phonetically regular (*in, is, and, can, went*) or irregular (*the, of, have, was, should*). All high-frequency words could, in fact, become sight words.

It makes sense to teach the high-frequency words students will encounter in text. Although it seems astounding, it is widely accepted that thirteen words account for approximately 25% of the text we encounter (Johns, J. and Wilke, K., Burkins, J. and Yates, K.). Furthermore, Burkins and Yates (2021) list 109 high-frequency words that account for more than 50% of the words that students will encounter in their reading (92).

Curious about those thirteen words? In alphabetical order: a, and, for, he, in, is, it, of, that, the, to, was, you.

Consider the power, then, in helping our students master these words. If students can read these words with automaticity, they can then devote more working memory to the many other demands of reading. Many teachers are not aware of these statistics; sharing this data can motivate teachers to ensure an intentional focus on these words in their classrooms.

Dolch and Fry High-Frequency Word Lists

Have you heard of the Dolch and Fry lists of words? Both lists contain high-frequency words that can be taught to students. The Dolch list was first published in 1936. It includes 220 words and is organized by grade level (Pre-K to Grade 3). The Dolch grade level lists do not include nouns; Dolch created a separate list of 95 high-frequency nouns.

The Fry list contains 1000 high-frequency words and was first published in 1957. This list contains words from all parts of speech, including nouns. The Fry words are organized into groups of 100, according to those most frequently used in print.

Because I had a background in literacy, as a teacher, I was aware of these lists. When I was an administrator, though, I realized that many teachers were not familiar with them, especially teachers without elementary training. Either set of words can be effective for reference and incorporated into instruction.

A Shift in Instructional Methods: Orthographic Mapping

It is important to remember that many high-frequency words are phonetic. Take, for example, this list of high-frequency words: *a, but, get, it, is, at, can, has, his, with.* All of these words are decodable. Teachers could be intentional about including these high-frequency words when they are teaching the corresponding phonemes: let the phonics do the work. Then, more time can be devoted to those high-frequency words that are irregular, words that students would not be able to decode with their phonetic knowledge. But how?

Many educators approach the teaching of high-frequency words through drill and repetition, hoping for memorization. Kilpatrick (2016) turns to research to support a shift in instruction: "Researchers have discovered the mental process we use to efficiently store words for instant, effortless retrieval. It is called *orthographic mapping*" (4). He continues,

> **Orthographic mapping** helps explain how words become familiar. If a word is "mapped" to permanent memory, it is a familiar word and instantly recognizable. No sounding-out or guessing is needed. If a word has not been "mapped," it is not familiar and needs to be identified in some other way. (6)

Orthographic mapping can be used with all words, whether they are phonetic or not, high-frequency or not. It is a process that is deliberate in mapping the word for meaning, sounds, and spelling, connecting it to various contexts to lock it into memory.

Let's look at an example of orthographic mapping with the word *have*:

1. Say the word to students and ask them to repeat it.

Today we're going to map the word have. *Say it with me.* Have.

2. Connect the word to meaning and/or give context.

We use this word a lot. Sometimes we use it in statements like this one: I have new shoes on today. *Sometimes we use it when we are asking questions:* Have you seen Min this morning?

3. Analyze the sounds in the word.

As I say the word have, *I want you to put up a finger for each sound you hear. I'll say it slowly:* h-a-ve.
How many sounds did you hear? That's right! Three.
Try saying the word yourself and put up a finger for each sound you hear. I should hear you stretching out that word.

4. Analyze the spelling of the word.

Okay, now I am going to write the word have *on the board. Look at the letters as I say each sound.*
What did you notice? (Students can talk about the letter *e* used at the end of the word.)
You're right. There is an e *at the end of the word* have. *What sound does the letter* e *usually make? /e/ Do we hear the /e/ sound in* have?

Orthographic mapping is new to many teachers. Do you have a teacher on staff familiar with the process? Could that individual model a lesson for your other teachers? If not, you might decide to use the example and script provided here to demonstrate orthographic mapping for your teachers.

5. **Connect the word's sounds with its spelling.**

   You told me there are three sounds in the word have. *Let's look at the letters that go with each sound.*

   Using an Elkonin box with three spaces, write the letters for the word *have* as you say it, stretching it out for emphasis. The last box will have *v* and *e* together as *ve*.

h	a	ve

   What did you notice about the letters? That's right! The letters v *and* e *are together making the /v/ sound.*

6. **Give students the opportunity to practice reading and spelling the word.** Individual whiteboards are ideal for this activity.

   Okay, you write the word with me now. Listen to the sounds as you write.
   Did you remember to put both letters v *and* e *for the /v/ sound? If not, add the* e *now.*
   Let's read it together. Drag your fingers under the letters as you read.
   Great! Now erase your board and try writing the word yourself.
   Once you're finished, read it one more time.

7. **Connect back to meaning and context.**

   A few minutes ago, I used the word have *in a statement—I have new shoes on today. Turn to your partner and say a statement using the word* have.
   I also used the word have *in a question—Have you seen Min this morning? Ask your partner a question using this word. Here's a hint: the word* have *will often be at the beginning of a question.*

8. **Connect to other words that follow a similar pattern.**

   Can you think of any other words that are spelled this way with the letters v *and* e *at the end making the /v/ sound?* (love, live)

   If there is time, map one of these other words as well.

This explicit mapping of the high-frequency word *have* will help lock the word into a student's memory. You might have noticed that words of a similar pattern can be addressed as well. Although teachers will not necessarily address all words in this way, this method has proven to have much more efficient transfer than traditional drill and practice.

Word Walls

I highly recommend word walls in elementary classrooms. The *way* they are used, however, is important. If students come into class for the first time at the beginning of the school year and the word wall is already full of words, it loses its usefulness immediately. Word walls are most effective when we build them *with* our students. If you look back at the weekly schedules in Chapter 3, you'll notice that I scheduled time for word walls every Monday. This is the time I introduce 2 to 4 new words to my class (the number determined by the grade and the words

"… orthographic mapping is a major discovery that should dramatically affect how we understand and teach reading" (Kilpatrick 2016, 5).

themselves) and together we add the words to the word wall. Look at the word walls in your classrooms. Are they established when students come into school at the beginning of the year, or are they being added to regularly?

Are there word walls in your classrooms? Do you ever see teachers or students referring to them during writing or instruction? As you look at the words, do you see potential patterns that teachers have been focusing on?

I am intentional about the groupings of the words I add. Sometimes I might choose high-frequency words I've noticed students spelling incorrectly in their writing: *could, should,* and *would* are an effective grouping. Sometimes I might choose words that all have blends reinforcing a previously taught phonetic concept: *when, which, what.* (Note: five of these six words are on Fry's First 100 high-frequency word list.) Regardless of which words I add, imagine the power of mapping those words orthographically with students. We wouldn't necessarily have to map all three words being introduced that week but if we map at least one, the impact will be noticeable.

I playfully refer to my word wall as my No-Excuse Word Wall. Once the word is on the wall, there's no excuse for spelling it wrong! The goal is to lock the spelling into students' long-term memory; those who need reminders, though, can refer to the wall during their writing. And if they know the word is on the wall, *and* they know I will send them back to fix that word, they learn to be sure about the spelling before handing something in.

When I was an administrator, I was often on supervision during lunch, walking from classroom to classroom. During this time, I sometimes played a word-wall game with students. I would begin by saying, "I'm thinking of a word on your word wall…" and then give clues, such as "that has a blend at the beginning of the word" or "that rhymes with _____" or "that has a silent letter at the end." Students would enjoy guessing which word I was thinking of without realizing my intention of drawing attention to their word wall!

Vocabulary Development

As we read in Chapter 4, vocabulary is part of overall language comprehension. The Science of Reading data has also suggested that it requires explicit instruction. Students learn an astounding number of new words on a daily basis. In fact, there are estimates that they learn between six and ten new words a day. How? Through both exposure and explicit teaching!

Consider your own vocabulary development as you read this book, especially this chapter! The understanding of the words and terminology provide a greater understanding of the concepts themselves. You might not remember the meaning of each word the first time you see it but, as you are exposed to it repeatedly and begin to use it yourself, your understanding deepens.

If we never hear or read new words, how will we ever learn them? In my experience, students love being challenged by new words and feel respected when we don't oversimplify things or talk down to them. Exposure to new words through our discussions and through read-alouds are particularly important. Consider the books read to students during language arts, perhaps, but in other subject areas, too. Our students will likely encounter many new words in these situations. Although they might not yet be able to decode them if reading on their own, when *we* read them, we provide the exposure they need. Then, through context and discussion, they will begin to understand them. They might not remember the meaning of words after a first exposure, though, so repeated exposure and some explicit teaching are most effective.

Consider how morphology can connect to new vocabulary being introduced. In math, students might be learning about triangles. Effective teachers can take the opportunity to teach the prefix *tri–*. This explicit teaching will help students access and understand other words, such as *tricycle, trike, triple, tripod.*

When I was a consultant and administrators were looking for an effective school-wide practice, I would often suggest a focus on vocabulary. It proved successful time and again. Before getting into the *how*, let's consider the *what*.

The Three Tiers of Vocabulary

Vocabulary words are sorted into three tiers. All three tiers of vocabulary are important to consider within our classrooms. Let's explore each tier.

Tier One Vocabulary

Examples of Tier One words: *chair, rain, walk, happy, clock.*

Tier One vocabulary includes words that are used most commonly in everyday conversation.

Most of our students come into school with these words already in place. The exception may be our English Language Learners or those with cognitive delays.

Tier Two Vocabulary

Examples of Tier Two words: *describe, list, explain, analyze, compare, evaluate.*

Tier Two vocabulary refers to academic words that cross disciplinary boundaries.

Academic vocabulary is essential in our classrooms. Sometimes, though, we neglect to teach these words explicitly to our students. We expect that students will know what we mean when we tell them to *analyze* the article or *categorize* those words. But have we ever discussed their meaning? Beck, McKeown, and Kucan (2013) have stated that "… instruction towards Tier Two words can be most productive" (9).

If students are assigned homework that includes Tier Two vocabulary (most school work does), it could be frustrating for those who do not understand the words used in the instructions. Without understanding the vocabulary in the questions, they would likely not be able to complete the work. And yet, they may well understand the content.

Tier Three Vocabulary

Examples of Tier Three words:
- *equation, fraction, sum, multiply*
- *herbivore, carnivore, species, habitat*
- *democracy, election, parliament, community*

Remember the use of pictures and questioning described in Chapter 4 on oral language? Intentional (content-area–related) picture choices will encourage students to use their vocabulary words in yet another context.

Tier Three vocabulary refers to discipline-specific words.

Without me specifying, I'm sure you are able to determine which subject area each group of words in the margin belongs to.

Typically, teachers are more explicit in teaching Tier Three words because they expect the words to be new to most students. Tier Three words are often grade-specific depending on curricular outcomes. Should these words be taught explicitly? Absolutely. In fact, they are often excellent words to examine for morphemes.

A school-wide focus is most effective with Tier Two words, or academic vocabulary. Why? Tier Two vocabulary is used at all grade levels, whereas Tier Three words are typically more specific to grade-level curriculum. As a staff, you might decide on ten Tier Two words that would be beneficial for students of all grade levels. Each month, one of those words becomes the focus. Each teacher would ensure the explicit teaching of that word in their classroom. The word could be highlighted on broadcast or during announcements, and posted on a hallway bulletin board, accessible to all. Classes could add evidence of learning to the bulletin board through their own writing, questions, or QR codes with video links. I have witnessed this in action in many schools. What a powerful experience to see students from all grade levels learning the same words: words that will be used throughout their academic careers. A unified teaching approach like this can also provide opportunities for administrators and literacy coaches to

If you decide to pursue this idea as a school-wide focus, as a staff you might want to explore Marzano's Six Step Process for teaching academic vocabulary.

In Chapter 7, we discuss how spelling influences our students' writing and why a careful approach within the context of writing is essential.

The topic of spelling tests is an effective one for a staff meeting, as teachers often have different approaches and perspectives on this topic. I have included questions to guide the conversation in the Talk Time reproducible on page 62.

meaningfully engage with students during instructional walks, on broadcast or morning announcements. Students enjoy sharing and celebrating their learning!

Even your Kindergarten students can engage in this learning. I have watched Kindergarten teachers explicitly teach words like *analyze* and *compare* to their students. They often use a simple definition, include an action to help students remember the word, and then have the students practice with that word repeatedly: in conversation and in action.

Teachers can also use strategies such as concept circles, mind mapping, word sorts, picture dictionaries, and personal dictionaries to support students with new vocabulary.

Spelling Tests: Yes or No?

When I was an administrator, I was surprised how many parents voiced their desire for weekly spelling tests in their children's classes. Yet traditional spelling tests are often quite meaningless, yielding little or no transfer for most students. Students score ten out of ten on Friday's test, but on Monday the same words are spelled incorrectly in their writing.

After reading this chapter, it likely becomes evident how our teachers should be approaching word study, including spelling, within their classrooms. If teachers plan on giving spelling tests, they should be grounded in word patterns, phonetics, morphology, or similarities between high-frequency words: anything to make the tests more meaningful and to increase the likelihood of transfer.

Instructional Walk Considerations: Word Study

After reading and thinking more about word study, consider these questions on your next instructional walk:

- In Kindergarten, is attention placed on phonological awareness, such as beginning, middle, and end sounds in words; rhyming words; clapping syllables; blending sounds to form words; segmenting words into individual sounds?
- Do Grade 1 and 2 students have an alphabet on their desks or tables for easy reference?
- Are your Grade 1 and 2 teachers intentional about the explicit instruction of phonemic awareness and phonics?
- What resources do teachers use to teach phonemic awareness and phonics? Do they follow an intentional scope and sequence?
- Are teachers at higher grade levels (especially in Grade 3 and above) teaching morphology (bases, roots, prefixes, suffixes) to their students?
- Do students have access to either a sound wall or a word wall in their classrooms? (Teachers should refer to these resources regularly for maximum effectiveness.)
- Is word study embedded in a variety of literacy contexts (read-alouds, think-alouds, literacy stations, guided reading) and in subject areas other than language arts?

Talk Time: Word Study

Choose a specific word study topic that is most timely for you, or discuss the set(s) of questions decided upon by your school team.

Phonemic Awareness and Phonics

> "Poor phonological awareness is the most common cause of poor reading. Reading problems can be *prevented* if all students are trained in letter-sound skills and phonological awareness, starting in Kindergarten." (Kilpatrick 2016, 13)

- How much phonemic awareness and phonics instruction occurs in your classroom? How do you incorporate this instruction into your day? What resource(s) do you use?
- If you teach the older grades, are there students who still need this instruction? If so, how do you provide it?
- Did you know that many struggling readers have difficulty rhyming, segmenting words, blending words? Why do you think this is?

Morphology

- What do you know about morphology?
- Do you incorporate morphology in your teaching? How?

Sight Words and High-Frequency Words

- What is the difference between sight words and high-frequency words? How might you explain the difference to a parent or colleague who asks?
- How do you teach these words to your students? Is it effective?
- Have you heard of orthographic mapping? Can you describe it to a colleague?

Vocabulary

Beck, McKeown, and Kucan (2013) have stated that "instruction towards Tier Two words can be most productive" (9). Tier Two vocabulary refers to academic words that cross disciplinary boundaries. Examples: *describe, list, explain, analyze, compare, evaluate.*

- Are you aware of the Three Tiers of Vocabulary? What do you know about them?
- How could you be more intentional about teaching Tier Two academic words to your students? Why might the teaching of Tier Two words be especially beneficial for students?
- How do you typically expose your students to new vocabulary words? Are you intentional in this process?

Spelling Tests

- Describe your students' spelling abilities.
- Do you give spelling tests to your students? If so, do you think they are effective? If not, are there ways to adapt them to make them more effective?
- How can you (or do you) assist students with conventional spelling? (In the earlier grades, invented spelling is acceptable, but we strive toward more conventional spelling.)

Pembroke Publishers ©2023 *Literacy Leadership Matters* by Karen Filewych ISBN 978-1-55138-361-3

6

Reading

"Reading is both a cognitive and an emotional journey."
— Donalyn Miller

Imagine… we have only now arrived at the chapter on reading, despite discussing it in every chapter prior to this. We have considered literacy goals, the importance of creating a school environment for reading, reading theories, the reading wars, prereading skills, and even what makes a skilled reader. You may be wondering what's left.

In Chapter 5, we outlined the five components that the Science of Reading data identified as requiring explicit instruction: *phonemic awareness, phonics, fluency, vocabulary,* and *comprehension*. We have already discussed phonemic awareness, phonics, and vocabulary; in this chapter we turn our attention to fluency and comprehension. And once again, although these components are separated for ease of discussion, it is critical to remember that they are inextricably woven together. We are also going to address the various instructional practices that we expect to see in elementary classrooms, discuss reading assessments and screeners, and examine some traditional practices. But first, let's explore the ideas of reader identity and the power of literature.

Developing Reader Identity

Developing reader identity is not solely the responsibility of the classroom teacher. Our decisions as administrators, our interactions with students, and even the school decor, can all contribute to our students' reader identity.

As elementary educators, one of our fundamental goals is to create proficient readers. In addition, though, we also want our students to identify themselves as readers. Why is this important? In *The Reading Mind*, Daniel Willingham (2017) explains the virtuous cycle of reading:

> … enjoyment means that you have a better attitude toward reading; that is, you believe that reading is a pleasurable, valuable thing to do. A better attitude means you read more often, and more reading makes you even better at reading—your decoding gets still more fluent, lexical representations become richer, and your background knowledge increases. We would also predict the inverse to be true: if reading is difficult you won't enjoy it, you'll have a negative attitude toward the activity, and you'll

avoid it whenever possible meaning that you'll fall still further behind your peers. (139)

I have witnessed this cycle with countless students. Unfortunately, even at a young age, many students develop negative associations with reading. We don't often know the specific experiences our students have with books and reading in the home, but we can speculate, based on the attitudes they bring to school. And the range is diverse. Some students walk into our schools already loving books, knowing their alphabet, perhaps already able to identify simple words; these students have likely been surrounded by books from a young age and have adults in their lives who read to them regularly. Other students walk into our schools with a curiosity about books and reading, and a rudimentary understanding of letters and words; they've had some exposure and they are excited for more. There are other students who walk into our schools with little or no exposure to books. Before long, these students recognize that they don't have the same understanding as their peers. They can't identify the specifics, of course, but they know there is a difference. Sometimes, this lack of understanding the **concepts of print** can lead to feelings of frustration.

These examples refer to our emergent readers. Fast forward a few years to a student in Grade 2, or 3, or 6: a student who still cannot easily access the words on the page, whose experience with reading has become even more than frustration—by now, defeat.

Is it any wonder, then, that our teachers need to get our students excited about books and reading? Why relationships are essential? Why building trust is essential? As Miller (2009) reminds us, "Reading is both a cognitive and an emotional journey" (16). When dealing with emotions, human relationships are critical.

Understanding the theories and the science behind how we learn to read is important. Arguably as important, though, are the needs, attitudes, and emotions of the students within our classrooms. We take the research, use it to inform best practice, set the foundation for our students, and prevent as many reading difficulties as we can. If we were to proceed with only the theories and the science in mind, we would be missing a crucial part of the teaching of reading: helping students develop a positive reader identity.

If you were to observe me teaching a lesson on reading, I would address the students in this way, "Okay, *readers*, today we are going to …" (The same is true when I am teaching a lesson on writing: "*Grade 1 writers*, I want you to notice …") Many emerging readers don't see themselves as readers; many older students don't see themselves as *skilled* readers. By referring to them in this way, my intent is to begin to shift their self-concept. Teaching reading is certainly more than science.

As an administrator, you might find opportunities to refer to your students as readers, too. If you walk into a classroom and everyone is reading, you might say, "Good morning, Grade 2 readers! Hands up and tell me what you are reading today." Of course, teachers would not be impressed if you interrupted their students' reading time every day, but occasionally this might be an opportunity to talk about books they are reading and favorites, while strengthening your students' reader identity.

The awareness of how print works is known as *concepts of print*: the understanding that text holds meaning, that letters form words, that print is read from top to bottom and from left to right, how pages are turned, and so on.

The Power of Literature

I am passionate about empowering students with the gift of literacy. There have been times during the writing of this book when I've felt like I should stand on a soapbox. This is one of those times. I cannot stress enough the importance of quality literature for our teachers and students. Have you ever taken the time to browse the books on the shelves of your classrooms or the school library? Sometimes you might be surprised at what you discover!

Literature holds such power. Elementary teachers have a wonderful opportunity to teach their students to read and write. Through this process, though, they also have the opportunity to help their students grow as people. Sometimes our world is not an easy place to live. We face complicated, confusing realities; our young students are not immune to this. In her book, *Better with Books*, Melissa Hart (2019) says,

> Life can be difficult for both fictional characters and real kids; conflict is, after all, inevitable in this business of living. But life is also a tremendous gift, full of wonder and excitement and opportunities to make powerful connections. With this in mind, we can give young readers literature that inspires and delights, that provides opportunities for thoughtful discussion and deliberate action, and that fosters empathy for the way they see themselves and others. (xix)

Teachers will be using books in various instructional contexts. Whatever the context, there should be a variety of genres and text forms available for use: fiction (picture books, beginning chapter books, graphic novels, novels, plays), nonfiction (informational texts, biographies, magazines, cookbooks, manuals), poetry, and digital text. As powerful as narrative texts can be, we must not rely on fiction at the expense of other genres. A balance is essential. In most provincial curricula, there are specific references to various genres and types of text that should be used in elementary classrooms. In the Alberta English Language Arts and Literature curriculum, for example, there is an entire section of outcomes devoted to text forms and structures. In the Ontario Language curriculum, the first section of outcomes related to reading refer to a variety of texts, the list specific to each grade level. There are subsequent sections devoted to text forms, text patterns, and text features.

"When the goal is to develop proficient, confident, joyful readers and writers, it's all about texts—the quality and quantity of meaningful, interesting texts that students can access." (Routman 2014, 95)

The resources we share with our students should be well-written, represent a mixture of current and classic, and reflect the diversity within our classrooms. Our students should see themselves reflected in the books they read. A critical eye is necessary when evaluating our resources with this lens. Are we including text with diverse characters? Are the books on our shelves written by diverse authors? If we have especially reluctant readers in our school, how will we hook them on books? What topics might entice them? Which authors? Do we have books written by authors that students have had personal contact with through an author visit?

This Tournament of Books project created countless opportunities for oral language development and data management as well.

Another powerful way to engage all students with a variety of literature is by choosing picture books that everyone in the school will read. I know of one school that held an incredibly successful year-long Tournament of Books. Staff decided on 16 books at the beginning of the year. The covers of the books were copied and placed in a tournament bracket on a central school bulletin board. Two books would go head to head, with the teachers reading them to their classes. After the classes had the opportunity to read both books, the students would vote on their favorite between the two. The winning book would proceed to the next bracket to face off with another book. This continued throughout the year until a favorite book was chosen!

Ultimately, it comes down to this: How can we choose and use literature in our schools to ensure that all of our students will identify themselves as readers?

Fluency

Have you ever held the microphone for a student at an assembly or during announcements and listened as they struggled to get through a sentence? Painful, isn't it? Because of the audience, these situations emphasize the need for fluency. But fluency is important for reading in any circumstance. Kilpatrick (2016) explains,

> For good readers, word reading is fluent. Fluent means fast and accurate, and includes proper expression. Fluent readers comprehend more of what they read because they can focus their attention on the meaning, not on figuring out the words. (3)

The focus on word recognition in Chapter 5 (phonics, morphology, sight words, high-frequency words, and orthographic mapping) all contribute to fluency, which in turn contributes to comprehension. When you hear that student reading word by word, attempting to figure out each word before tackling the next, the reading sounds quite choppy. By the time the student gets to the end of the sentence, there is little chance of remembering the words to construct meaning from the sentence, particularly as sentence lengths increase. Such a student will not be able to read with expression or **prosody**, except through many repeated readings.

Prosody refers to the ability to read with expression, including elements such as phrasing, pitch, rhythm, intonation, tone, and emphasis.

If you find yourself in a situation in which students will be reading aloud to the school, during an assembly or announcements, give them time to practice even as you wait. We shouldn't assume this has already been done, and often nerves are a factor, too. Set up students for success by asking them read the text aloud a few times, or by having them listen to you read it out loud.

Are your teachers familiar with Scarborough's Reading Rope (see pages 39–40) and the many strands involved in being a skilled reader?

How do we improve fluency? Chapter 5 leads us in the right direction: our students need word recognition with as much automaticity as possible. In addition, students learn fluency and prosody by listening to skilled readers (read-alouds) and then practicing together (shared reading through nursery rhymes, poetry, morning messages, choral reading, readers theatre—all are ideal opportunities to play with language). Lessons on the specific functions of punctuation, including commas, periods, question marks, exclamation marks, and quotation marks, all assist with fluency as well.

Students should understand that fluency is improved through multiple readings of the same text. Sometimes teachers encounter negative attitudes from students (and parents) about reading something a second or third time; yet this should become the norm in our classrooms. Not only will it improve fluency, but comprehension as well! Choral reading and readers theatre are effective practices to help improve fluency because they encourage rereadings of the same text. In the upcoming sections on instructional practices, we will explore other ways to make multiple readings of text more authentic.

Comprehension

How can you support your teachers in teaching reading comprehension? After all, isn't comprehension the ultimate goal of reading? We wouldn't engage in reading behavior if it didn't yield some result. Whether the text is meant to entertain, inform, or instruct, the end goal remains the same: comprehension.

As we have explored at length, there are many other skills that must be in place before adequate comprehension occurs. Think back to Scarborough's Reading Rope from pages 39–40. If a student is struggling with comprehension, it is worth taking time to determine if one of the smaller strands of the rope is the stumbling block. Read this example and then consider the necessary focus of instruction for this student.

> … when a beginning reader uses the letter-sound translation process (i.e., sounds a word out), her working memory is occupied mostly by translation rules—"let's see, 'o' usually sounds like aw, but when there are two of them, 'oo,' they make a different sound… what was it again?" That leaves little working memory space for the task of comprehension, for actually understanding the meaning of what she's read. (Willingham, 2017, 65)

So although it is true that this student is not comprehending what she is reading, it has become clear that the focus for this student should be on word recognition: specifically phonemic awareness and orthographic mapping. This serves as a reminder that the explicit teaching of phonemic awareness, phonics, vocabulary, and fluency work together toward comprehension of text.

Willingham (2017) says,

> … reading comprehension seems to be composed of three processes. The reader (1) extracts ideas from sentences, (2) connects these ideas to one another, and (3) builds some more general idea of what the text is about. (107)

When it is described this way, I am reminded that this skill, too, is more complicated than it first appears.

You may choose to provide your teachers with a copy of the Systems of Strategic Actions diagram which can be found on the inside cover of *The Literacy Continuum* by Fountas and Pinnell (2016). Keeping it close at hand might remind them of the various processes and questions to engage in with students to ensure adequate comprehension.

There are various elements of comprehension to consider. Fountas and Pinnell created what they call the Systems of Strategic Actions. They developed a graphic to show the complex thinking required for readers to meaningfully engage in text. They divided the graphic into three ways of thinking:

1. Thinking Within the Text
   - Searching for and Using Information
   - Monitoring and Self-Correcting
   - Solving Words
   - Maintaining Fluency
   - Adjusting
   - Summarizing
2. Thinking Beyond the Text
   - Predicting
   - Making Connections
   - Synthesizing
   - Inferring
3. Thinking About the Text
   - Analyzing
   - Critiquing

Each of these sections outlines specific processes that readers engage in with text. I have found this diagram useful for helping teachers guide their students to meaningful comprehension. The first section—Thinking Within the Text—focuses on the literal meaning of a text, an essential component of comprehension. The second section—Thinking Beyond the Text—helps students understand what they are reading more deeply. They make connections to their background knowledge, their own experiences, and their current understanding of the world to arrive at a new, revised understanding. The third section—Thinking About the Text—is one that many teachers have admitted they often neglect, unintentionally, of course. It is here that we think about the author, the text type, the purpose of the text, and the intentional decisions made by the author (the writer's craft). All of these elements are critical for accurate comprehension.

If you are observing teachers discussing the comprehension of text with students, see if you can determine which type of questions they are asking most frequently: Thinking *Within, Beyond,* or *About* the Text. Teachers are not always aware of their tendencies.

Thinking about and understanding text beyond the literal meaning is essential. If students understand the literal meaning of what they read but cannot make connections to their own lives, the meaning generated from the text is somewhat superficial. These students may not experience the joy or emotional connection that comes from reading a book. As another example, students might understand the literal meaning of the sentence "I love broccoli!" and yet not have the ability to infer the tone of the sentence based on context clues. This is especially challenging for our English Language Learners.

Teachers can assist their students with comprehension through

- thinking aloud during read-alouds and shared reading
- discussion (before, during, and after reading) as a whole class
- turn-and-talk opportunities
- reader response writing (which we will discuss in more detail in the next chapter)

How might you discuss or model one or more of these strategies during a staff meeting?

As always, it is most effective if students are aware of the specific processes and strategies involved in their thinking during reading. Teachers should be using the language of comprehension with their students—summarizing, predicting, inferring, analyzing—to help students recognize the processes at work.

Instructional Practices to Support Reading

Whatever it is we are doing as teachers, we should be doing so with purpose. There are not enough instructional minutes in a day to do things "just because." If our ultimate goal for reading is comprehension, and we know all the factors that lead to comprehension, we must be intentional to help our students reach that goal. As you will see, each of these instructional practices serves a purpose. In fact, you'll notice that each of the instructional practices fall within a stage of the gradual release of responsibility.

Read-Alouds

All these instructional practices can (and should) be used with *all* elementary grade levels! Watch for them on your instructional walks.

The role of read-alouds in our classrooms cannot be underestimated. Presumably, your teacher is the best reader in the room. Students need to hear effective, fluent reading. An effective reader uses variations in tone, pace, intonation, volume, and expression to convey meaning. Without hearing effective reading, students don't know what to strive for or have anything to mimic.

Read-alouds serve many other purposes, too: exposure to text above the independent reading level of the students, a variety of genres, and new vocabulary. They are often the heart of a mini-lesson, providing opportunities for the teacher to think aloud and demonstrate their own processes at work. Read-alouds can also spark interesting discussion and provide opportunities to practice oral language skills. Teachers can stop as often or little as they'd like during a read-aloud, depending on the focus of that day's lesson. Teachers do not engage in read-alouds purely for pleasure, although hopefully this is a consistent by-product of the process.

When I was a consultant, I had a teacher contact me in tears. Her administrator told her she was doing too many read-alouds. She was devastated and asked how she was supposed to teach without read-alouds. I quickly reassured her that reading aloud to her students was sound pedagogy and important for their reading development. Read-alouds will occur daily in elementary classrooms, sometimes even twice a day. Watching an effective teacher reading aloud to students—and the many instructional moves made in the process—can be enlightening, as there is so much at work during this instructional practice.

Within the gradual release of responsibility, read-alouds are often part of the explicit instruction: *I do!*

Shared Reading

During shared reading, students and teacher read together. Most often, the text is projected on the interactive whiteboard. The teacher may read a portion of the text and then invite the students to read along too. Sometimes, the teacher might ask students to take over entirely. When we consider the gradual release of responsibility, we recognize that, at this stage, there is still some teacher support, as much or as little seems to be needed: *We do!*

Shared reading often occurs within a mini-lesson to reinforce in context the concept being taught. For example, during a lesson on pacing, we cannot simply talk about the idea of using punctuation to guide our reading. Students must practice: practicing first with teacher support is ideal. (Students at all grade levels

Imagine the delight of a class if one day they discover that the morning message is from you instead of their teacher!

benefit from a lesson such as this.) Shared reading can also occur during activities like choral reading or readers theatre. Primary teachers can use this instructional practice daily with their morning message.

Guided Reading

I have seen guided reading mandated by administrators in various ways: a particular number of groups or minutes each day. If guided reading is something you want all your teachers to be engaged in during the week, talk to them about what is reasonable for their grade level. Refer back to the sample weekly schedules. Yes, this small-group instruction is embedded in the weekly schedule, but not at the expense of other instructional practices.

Guided reading provides an opportunity for targeted instruction to meet the varying instructional needs of students. Teachers work with small groups of students and differentiate instruction for each group. Although it would be ideal to meet with all students in this context on a regular basis, classroom realities compel us to prioritize. We meet with those students who are struggling more often than those who are flying.

During guided reading, the teacher leads students through intentional prereading strategies (looking at the cover, making predictions about the text/genre, discussing challenging vocabulary) and discussion. The teacher also focuses on a specific skill or strategy that is needed for this particular group of students. Then, all students begin reading silently to themselves, practicing what has just been taught. The teacher takes the time to listen to each student read a portion of the book, and perhaps have a quick discussion before moving on to the next student.

Guided reading is sometimes misunderstood. I have noticed that some teachers ask one student to read while the others listen to their peer. This is not the intention of guided reading and not an efficient use of time. These students need practice reading. The objective is for each of them to practice and engage with the text, not to listen to each other read. The teacher listens to each student read aloud; the others continue to read quietly at their own pace until it is their turn to read aloud to the teacher.

Guided reading is an opportunity to hand responsibility over to the students and provide scaffolding only as needed *(We do!)*. Writing about guided reading, Routman (2014) says,

> … we need to be cautious about providing too much support, such as spending too much time on prereading activities or giving students all the "answers" so that we wind up doing most of the reading work. (132)

Although we are there to support our students, this is the opportunity for them to take calculated risks and practice in a smaller, less threatening environment.

Timing

Short, intentional sessions are the most efficient use of time for guided reading, and 15 to 20 minutes is usually enough. One of the most important considerations when teachers are engaged in a guided reading session with a small group of students is what the other students in the class are doing. After all, this instructional time should be valuable for all. Careful planning is therefore essential. The other students in the class should be able to work productively, either independently or in small groups, during this time. Teachers know this is easier said than done. Even 15 to 20 minutes of independent work takes much training and practice, especially with a dynamic class or behavior concerns. If your teachers are not engaged in a lot of guided reading at the beginning of the year, this is likely the reason: it takes time to establish routines and ensure accountability during independent work.

During your instructional walks, you might notice that teachers are taking the time to establish these routines: this is something to acknowledge and celebrate!

Groupings

An appropriate group size for guided reading is 3 to 5 students, certainly no more. Sometimes students are grouped according to level. However, the groups can also be more dynamic. Through observations and informal assessments, teachers can make note of which students need reinforcement with a particular skill or strategy. Then, for that day, those students come together for guided reading. In fact, they don't have to be reading at the same level. If the intent is to reinforce a lesson on text features, for example, each student would need a nonfiction book at their own level (or slightly above) that includes the text features explored during the lesson. The same would be true (students reading books of different levels) for many objectives, such as reading with expression or paying attention to punctuation.

On occasion, I have noticed some administrators dictate which students should be engaged in guided reading and for how many sessions each week. I have also observed situations where teachers were asked to hand in a list of their guided reading groups. The intention was to hold teachers accountable. Keep in mind, however, that flexible, dynamic groupings will ensure all students get support when they need it. Struggling readers might be receiving intervention support outside of the classroom which can then provide teachers with an opportunity to work with others who need a little boost through intentional scaffolding. Also, the groupings can change, based on the skills being taught.

Paired Reading/Reading Buddies

Paired reading, sometimes known as partner reading, is another instructional practice that can be effective. This can certainly be done within a classroom, but here I want to address how cross-grade pairings can bring more authenticity to the process. Reading buddies can be another way of providing practice during the gradual release of responsibility (*You do it together!*).

As a teacher, regardless of the grade I was teaching, I paired my students with another class. Perhaps my Grade 1 students were paired with Grade 6 students, or my Grade 5 students with Grade 3 students. These cross-grade connections are powerful when the time is used effectively. When I was an administrator, we often asked teachers to pair off with another class at the beginning of the year to ensure everyone had a buddy class.

Working with reading buddies gives us an opportunity to "show off" (i.e., practice) what we have been learning. For example, if we have been working on improving our fluency by paying attention to punctuation, then I remind my Grade 1 students that this is what they are demonstrating for their Grade 6 buddies. Knowing they are going to read to their buddies is a motivating reason to practice. Perhaps the Grade 6 students have been working on fluency, too, but with more complexity (pacing, phrasing, pitch, intonation, and expression). The Grade 6 teacher then reminds their students to practice their fluency as they read to the Grade 1 students. They choose a book to read to their buddies from the library beforehand. The Grade 6 teacher might even have them practice reading it once through before reading it to their buddies. This becomes a meaningful way for students to practice in an authentic context a skill they have been working on. Think about how many times they might reread the text!

Time with reading buddies could be scheduled every few weeks or once a month. This routine reinforces the learning relationship and capitalizes on the students' need to prepare and practice for their buddies.

I intentionally use reading buddies as a way to practice oral language skills, too. The students and I talk about how to connect with our buddies: what could we say to begin, what is polite, what we might say when the time is finished. I also use the opportunity to have my students articulate what they have been learning. If the focus for the Grade 1 students has been using punctuation to guide their reading, as in the example above, these are some examples of what students would say to their buddies before they begin reading: "We've been practicing stopping at the periods." "We use punctuation like street signs to guide our reading." "We can read more fluently when we pay attention to punctuation." You'll notice, their answers tend to reveal their level of understanding.

If you decide to establish reading buddies for all students in your school, it is worth a discussion with teachers to set expectations and talk about how the time can be used effectively. If I neglected to have this discussion with my teachers, I noticed that sometimes the instructional time was not valued. Some teachers, and therefore some students, saw it simply as time for socializing. There was no explicit intention, transitions took quite long, and the time was often wasted. It's not that the social component is not important; it is. In fact, these relationships can become quite significant and meaningful to students. When Grade 2 students notice their partners in the hallway and bubble over with excitement when their buddies say hello, we witness a wonderful by-product of this learning relationship. I have noticed that sometimes reading buddy classes plan their class parties together!

In one of my Grade 6 classes, there were a few students whose behavior was sometimes questionable. And yet, when I watched them with their younger reading buddies, I was surprised and quite honestly moved by the ways in which they interacted. I saw a different side of the students in these situations and, over time, these positive interactions helped improve their overall behavior. If you find yourself in an elementary/junior high, the junior-high students could also be involved. As a friend and colleague of mine has shared: "Some junior-high students are transformed into their best selves when a Grade 1 student is snuggled up against them reading their letters to Santa!"

Independent Reading

As we discussed in Chapter 1, independent reading should be part of the daily routine. When we think back to the gradual release of responsibility, we are working toward our students independently practicing the skills we have been teaching, ultimately leading to transfer. If we don't give students this time to practice, the reality is that many students will not read in other situations. What's interesting, though, is that when we do give our students time to read in class, if we approach things right, they will also be motivated to read in other situations of their choosing, including at home.

Make a point of walking around the school during independent reading at various times throughout the year. What do you notice? Are students engaged? Are they using the time as intended? If not, how could you approach this and problem-solve as a staff? Use the information in the upcoming sections to guide your decisions and your discussion with teachers.

What Should Students Be Reading?

Choice is essential. This is when our classroom libraries become especially important. Are there books on the shelves that will entice all of our students? Is

Which grade levels you pair together doesn't matter as much as how the time is used. You may even decide to use the term *learning partners* instead of *reading buddies* to reflect what you want out of the experience. Perhaps the staff could be part of this decision. *Reading buddies* has a pleasant connotation: as long as teachers respect the expectations of the time, it might be perfectly fine.

there a wide range of genres, authors, levels, and topics? Miller (2009) speaks of the benefits of choice:

> Providing students with the opportunity to choose their own books to read empowers and encourages them. It strengthens their self-confidence, rewards their interests, and promotes a positive attitude toward reading by valuing the reader and giving him or her a level of control. Readers without power to make their own choices are unmotivated. (23)

Indeed, some students will dive into anything; others could gravitate to one genre over another; others still might have never found a book they love. Typically, at the beginning of the year, teachers will talk to their students about making selections for independent reading. This is time well-spent if we consider how it can influence independent reading each and every day of the school year. It is important for students to realize that each of us is unique in terms of both interest and ability. We want all our students comfortable choosing what they are *interested* in reading and what they are *capable* of reading. An environment of trust and respect is therefore essential, especially for our most reluctant readers.

I don't want students choosing a book they think they should be reading (but can't), and then engage in what Donalyn Miller (and others) refer to as *fake reading*. You've seen it, I'm sure. A student has a book open in front of them. They turn the page after a reasonable amount of time. Their eyes may even scan the text every so often. But we know they're not actually reading. We don't want fake readers in our classrooms; we want engaged readers. Some students will do everything possible to avoid reading during independent reading time—they take an awfully long time choosing a book, insist on a bathroom break, or finally clean up the crayons they spilled in their desk. I see these students as a challenge: I want every student engaged in reading and I will do what it takes to engage them.

As a teacher, I have my students fill out an interest inventory or reading interest survey to get a sense of their topics of interest and preferred genres. If I notice a student who seems especially reluctant or indecisive during independent reading time, I am quick to talk to this student to help them find something of interest and something at their ability level. Bright (2021) refers to this process as *guided choice*. Some students might need teacher support to help them find the right fit, especially at first. We also shouldn't underestimate the power of book buzz! When the teacher (or the administrator) is sharing a favorite book or author, or talking about what they read over the weekend, this will generate excitement surrounding books.

What Should the Teacher Be Doing?

At the beginning of the year, especially, I encourage teachers to read during independent reading time. This sets an example and students come to understand that we value this time. They realize it is not time to organize their desks, talk to their friends, or ask the teacher a question. It is reading time for everyone. As the year goes on, teachers may take the opportunity to slide in beside a student and do a running record or engage in a short reading conference while everyone else is reading independently. In fact, students might look forward to their turn with the teacher. These activities still place the teacher right in the mix of the reading.

Kate Roberts (2018) says, "When kids get to choose their own books, they read more." (17)

Imagine this: You are surrounded by a wide variety of books and text types. But every day someone tells you what you must read. It is not your preferred genre. In fact, it doesn't excite or engage you at all. Would you bother reading that text, or would you engage in fake reading behaviors? You answer is likely the same as mine…

But if a teacher is always doing something else during independent reading time—grading, organizing field-trip forms, or talking to the teacher next door—students might interpret this time as filler and not essential. Modelling is key.

Reading Assessments

Many teachers have spent an inordinate amount of time giving reading assessments to their students. As I mentioned in Chapter 5, one of the practices that became common when balanced literacy was introduced was reading assessments in the form of DRA or benchmark assessments.

What is problematic about these assessments? Time. It is not an exaggeration to say that benchmark assessments can take anywhere between 15 to 60 minutes per student. With 25 students in a class, that's a lot of time for the students to be working independently rather than with teacher support. This is instructional time, don't forget. Many schools or districts had expectations for these assessments to be completed with every student multiple times throughout the year: sometimes twice, sometimes even three times. It's important to realize that these expectations were put in place with good intentions, based on common practices and understandings at the time. And yet, too often, the extensive time spent giving the tests was more to fill an obligation by the school or district, and less to inform instruction.

Can these assessments be useful? Absolutely. But they can be used with students that a teacher deems at risk, or a student they want to understand better as a reader. When completed in this way and in this context, the results can be used effectively to enhance instruction for the student.

It is, of course, important to understand where each student is at: their strengths and their stumbling blocks. Are there ways to monitor our students' reading that are not as time consuming? Thankfully, yes!

Running Records

Taking running records is one component of the benchmark assessments mentioned earlier. However, teachers can take quick running records with individual students without the formal benchmark assessment, simply by using a piece of paper and listening to students read. While my students were reading independently, I would slide in beside a student and listen to them read, completing a quick running record as they did. This would give me an idea of not only where they were at, but also what they might need to work on. I could also ask them a few questions to get a sense of their comprehension.

If some of your teachers are unsure of how to take these quick running records, access a district consultant or check to see if someone on staff is comfortable teaching the process to their colleagues.

Reading Screeners

One of the most efficient ways of getting to know our students as readers and identifying areas that require more attention is through reading screeners. There are several tools on the market that have become quite popular. One of the advantages of these screeners is that many of them can be given to the whole class at a time. And the ones that must be given individually take far less time than benchmark assessments. There are screeners designed to screen everything from phonemic awareness, to word reading, to oral reading fluency, to comprehension.

Check with your district consultants to see which screeners are commonly used in your area. Here are a few to reference as a starting point: DIBELS (Dynamic Indicators of Basic Early Literacy Skills), TOWRE (Test of Word Reading Efficiency), TOSWRF (Test of Silent Word Reading Fluency), and TOSREC (Test of Silent Reading Efficiency and Comprehension). In their book *This Is How We Teach Reading … And It's Working!*, Heather Willms and Giacinta Alberti (2022) provide quite a number of simple screeners that can be used with Kindergarten to Grade 3 students.

Screening tools are not meant as a summative assessment to be reported on to parents. They help us identify who is at risk and provide insight into appropriate instruction and/or intervention.

Re-examining Traditional Practices

Why do we do what we do? Is it because of the instructional merit of the practice? Or, sometimes, is it because we're in our comfort zone, doing what we've always done? I have slipped into this comfort zone on occasion. Re-examining traditional practices can ensure that teachers are making sound pedagogical decisions and doing what's in the best interest of our students.

Watch for the practices discussed in this section in your classrooms. If you see them happening, consider how you can approach teachers in a nonthreatening way to have them reflect on their practice. If you notice the same thing occurring in many classrooms, how might you bring up this practice at a staff meeting for discussion? Bear in mind that teachers are often quite passionate about what they do. Both our tone and our approach are essential considerations leading up to these discussions. It's not about being accusatory or judgmental; it's about best practice. If you do have a discussion during a staff meeting, consider sharing the appropriate section of this text with your teachers as a starting point. To help with tone, be sure you make clear that you are talking about a teaching practice, not about a person.

Round-Robin Reading

Most of us remember round-robin reading. What is it? When reading a shared text (in language arts or from a textbook in another subject), students are expected to read a paragraph or two out loud to the class before the next student takes over. In my experience, the teacher would often have the next person in the row read the next passage (even the idea of students in rows reflects a different era). As a student, I remember counting the paragraphs, figuring out which sentences I would be reading, and skimming the text beforehand. All this while others were reading aloud. Was I paying attention to content? Not at all. I was too fixated on my own upcoming turn to read. And once I had my turn, there seemed to be no need to pay attention. Was I the only student who coped with round-robin reading in this way? Most certainly not. As evident from my experience as a student, this practice is not pedagogically sound for many reasons.

If our goal is comprehension of the text, round-robin reading is not the answer. What can be done instead? Consider the instructional practices we have already

Willms and Alberti (2022) suggest, "An effective screen should be quick and targeted, taking no more than ten to fifteen minutes per student." (23)

In the Talk Time section of this chapter on page 79, there are some questions that might help you proactively engage in these discussions with teachers.

discussed. The teacher reading aloud, shared reading, and even partner reading would all be much more effective and maintain the dignity of our readers.

If, for some reason, we do want our students to read aloud to the class or school (during an assembly, for example), they should be given the passage ahead of time so they have ample time to practice reading the text. This is no different from the courtesy that we would extend to our own staff members in a similar situation.

Reading Logs

The purpose of reading logs is to track minutes or pages read, either during independent reading or home reading. Teachers often use them as a sort of accountability, proof of a student's reading. If students are reading in front of me, I have the proof I need. If they're reading at home, we have no actual proof. Even if we ask for a parent signature, there's no guarantee that the parents saw their child reading. And really, students could write down any number of minutes. I've also seen the requirement of a parent signature become problematic for some students, further disrupting an already difficult home relationship. There are also those students who read voraciously and become annoyed at having to complete the log. And if I know this student is reading, why the log?

Ultimately, it comes down to our goal: motivating our students to read. Will the log help motivate them? For most, probably not. If you have individual students who are motivated by the minutes they read (compare this to an exercise tracker for adults), then certainly let those students keep track (and set their own goals). But for most, reading logs are not worth the time or energy. Sometimes they even become a stressor, certainly not contributing to the joy of reading.

Incentive Programs (School-wide or Classroom-based)

Incentive programs are created with good intentions: get students reading! How do they work? Typically, there is a minute-goal for individual readers, or sometimes for the class. If students reach those minutes, they earn some kind of reward. Although this sounds reasonable on the surface, I have watched students reach their minute goal and then decide they've read enough for the week or the month. These students were obviously reading for the reward and not enjoying reading as the reward itself. Willingham (2017) offers this perspective,

> Rewards do work, at least in the short term. If you find a reward that the child cares about, he will read in order to get it. The problem is that you don't get the attitude boost we've predicted. In fact, the attitude is often less positive because of the reward. (149)

Miller (2009) concurs:

> Unfortunately, the only purpose these programs serve is to convince students there is no innate value in reading and that it is only worth doing if there is a prize attached. (150)

There are other ways to motivate students to read that yield more lasting results. When we generate book buzz in our schools, students are excited to pick up a book. When we surround them with an environment of books—books at their level, books they're allowed to take home and bring back, books that we can talk about—they discover the joy that reading can bring. When we allow students to choose what to read, they realize how reading can transport them to other times and places, real and fictional, or how they can learn more about their interests or idols.

Could we still hold a monthly draw for a pizza lunch where the winners get to read with the principal? Of course! But everyone in the school can be included in this draw, and it is not connected to how much has been read.

Whole-Class Novel Studies

As a student, did you ever experience a novel study with the whole class reading the same book? Were you able to read the book? Did you read it? Whether or not the experience was positive for you, there's a good chance that it wasn't positive for every student. During traditional novel studies, students are all reading the same book (regardless of their reading ability and with no differentiation). There are often pages upon pages of comprehension questions, quizzes on the details, and round-robin reading, all over an awfully long period of time. We now recognize that this practice is not pedagogically sound and is also quite intimidating for many students.

Sometimes, teachers choose novels to read aloud to their class, not as an official novel study, but simply as their read-aloud. This is not the process we are referring to in this section.

If you have teachers planning to do a whole-class novel study, I highly recommend that they read *A Novel Approach* by Kate Roberts to ensure they are planning appropriately and supporting their students' needs. If they ask for class sets of novels, this is your cue to have a deeper conversation about the practice and how they intend to approach it.

On the other hand, some of my favorite memories as a teacher surround the shared reading and discussion of a novel. When students erupt in laughter or are moved to tears during our reading of *Charlotte's Web, The One and Only Ivan, Wonder,* or *The Miraculous Journey of Edward Tulane,* I know that there is value in the experience. Is the shared reading of a novel the problem then? Not at all. The problem is the approach.

In her book, *A Novel Approach,* Kate Roberts (2018) says, "Guiding students through a whole-class novel can be a powerful experience for everyone in the room" (11). She continues,

> Having the support of a teacher and a class of peers when reading a book can lift the level of our thinking and can hold our attention in ways that sometimes reading on our own does not. (11)

There are other benefits of a shared novel experience:

- Students gain exposure to diverse texts or genres they might not choose on their own.
- Our community of learners is strengthened, providing us with common realizations and reference points throughout the school year.
- Students journey together through difficult content and sometimes difficult text.
- Our students share their own interpretations and opinions, often pushing the thinking of their peers.
- It provides many opportunities to improve oral language communication.

What can teachers do to ensure they don't fall into trap of traditional novel studies? In short, choose the right book, consider the pacing (less is more), differentiate throughout the process, ensure that most of the reading is done *during* class time, and plan the delivery methods carefully (some of the text will be read as your read-aloud, some through partner reading, and some during independent reading). Expecting all students to read the book independently (regardless of their ability), analyzing every page of text, and giving mounds of comprehension questions is not the way to go.

A whole-class novel experience, when done right, is powerful. And yet it is *one* instructional practice and should not be used at the exclusion of others. In elementary classrooms, I wouldn't recommend spending more than about three weeks on one book. Even with all the benefits this experience provides, students will want to choose their next read.

Instructional Walk Considerations: Reading

After reading and thinking more about the teaching of reading, consider these questions on your next instructional walk:

- Are your teachers reading aloud to their students daily? Are they reading quality texts in a variety of subject areas?
- Are there intentional conversations that occur before, during, or after read-alouds?
- Does the teacher use think-aloud strategies during read-alouds and shared reading?
- Is guided reading a regular practice in your classrooms?
- While the teacher is with one group for guided reading, what are the other students doing? Is the instructional time valuable for all?
- Do you see the benefit of establishing cross-grade reading buddies within your school? How might you facilitate this?
- Are there reading logs and reward programs in your school? Are they working?
- Do your teachers use novels for whole-class novel experiences? How are they engaging all students and differentiating for the varying needs in the classroom?

Talk Time: Reading

Take some time to read and think about this quotation and these questions before discussing them with your colleagues. Choose a specific topic about reading that is most timely for you, or discuss the set(s) of questions decided upon by your school team.

"Reading is both a cognitive and an emotional journey." Donalyn Miller

- How do you connect to this quotation by Donalyn Miller? How do you see this idea at work in your classroom?

Fluency and Comprehension

- How do you help your students improve their fluency? What specific strategies do you find effective?
- How do you help your students improve their comprehension? What specific strategies do you find effective?
- What do you find challenging about teaching fluency and comprehension?

Instructional Practices

- How often do you read aloud to your students? Do you choose books with a purpose in mind? Do you use books as mentor texts to teach a particular skill?
- Knowing we all have our own favorites and tendencies, how could you expand your classroom library, read-aloud, and shared reading material? Are there any genres or author groups you might be unintentionally neglecting?
- What are the benefits and challenges of guided reading? How might these challenges be addressed?
- Does your class have cross-grade reading buddies? What do you do with your reading buddies? How might you make this time more intentional and beneficial for both the younger and older buddies?

Rethinking Traditional Practices

- Do your students record their reading minutes in reading logs? Is this practice effective for all students?
- Do you have a reward program for reading? Does this motivate students to read and promote a love of reading? In the short term? The long term?
- Do you lead your students through whole-class novel experiences? What do you do to ensure that all students can access the text? How long do you spend on one book? What do you enjoy about this experience?

Pembroke Publishers ©2023 *Literacy Leadership Matters* by Karen Filewych ISBN 978-1-55138-361-3

7

Writing

"Be bold in the face of the blank sheet."
— Colum McCann

Why Teach Writing?

Just as I want to motivate and empower students to read beyond the four walls of my classroom, the same is true for writing. I don't want students to see writing purely as something they do for school. It is essential that they realize—from the earliest grade levels—that writing is a skill that will empower them to function more fully in the world, a skill they will use throughout their lives. They won't all be authors, but the ability to write will significantly increase their opportunities to be literate, functioning members of society. Statistically, individuals with low literacy skills have a higher probability of unemployment, incarceration, and living in poverty. Let's provide all students with the opportunity and motivation to write!

At the beginning of the year, one of my first activities with students is a brainstorm about reasons to read and write in the world. Why do we need these skills? Typically, we brainstorm in small groups and the students record their thoughts on chart paper. Then we engage in a *gallery walk*: groups of students walk around the room to read the ideas of other groups. Students are free to add to their own brainstorming as they see other ideas from their peers. Eventually, we engage in a large-group discussion. This lesson helps set the purpose for the year. Students are not learning to read and write more effectively for me, their teacher; they are learning to read and write more effectively for themselves, because reading and writing are skills they will use every day of their lives. Understanding the *why* changes students' views on what we are doing and also enhances their metacognition.

Similar to oral language, writing has two functions in our classrooms. Students must *learn to write*: our language arts curricula include many outcomes on writing. But students can also *write to learn*: constructing meaning in all areas of the curriculum. This chapter will focus on learning to write, which tends to occur primarily in our language arts classrooms. The next chapter, Literacy in the Content Areas, will address writing as a form of thinking, or writing to learn.

Could this activity be one you engage in with staff near the beginning of the year? It might very well be eye-opening for you and some of your teachers.

Even as I began writing this chapter, I wondered how I could possibly keep the teaching of writing—my greatest passion—to one chapter. I have limited the information here to what is vital to you, as an administrator, to help support your teachers. If you are interested in going deeper, my first two books, *How Do I Get Them to Write?* and *Freewriting with Purpose* (Pembroke Publishers), go into much more detail.

To help teachers work together on the skill of writing and alleviate some of the *blame game*, it can be beneficial to work toward a common school goal for writing.

At the beginning of my in-services on the teaching of writing, I ask teachers this question: *Do you assign written tasks to your students or do you teach your students how to write?* Sometimes I hear an audible reaction in the room when I pose this question: "Hmmm… I never thought of it like that." When we engage in discussion, it becomes clear that many teachers assign written tasks. I know I used to. It also becomes clear that teachers often feel ill-equipped to teach writing to their students because they are not writers themselves. I am passionate about empowering teachers to feel more confident about understanding the writing process and teaching writing to their students.

Through my conversations with teachers at all levels, I have heard how overwhelmed many of them are with the task of teaching students the craft of writing, a reality they are often hesitant to share with their administrators. Teaching writing is challenging; when principals recognize these challenges, teachers may feel more comfortable asking for support.

In my various roles, I have heard teachers lament the lack of writing skills that students arrive with in their classrooms, regardless of the grade they teach. Common observations: *They can't spell. They are reluctant to write. They won't revise or edit their work. They write the bare minimum. The writing lacks creativity.*

In elementary schools, we have a marvelous opportunity to instill positive perspectives on writing… To empower our student writers so they have the confidence to take risks… To provide them with skills and strategies… To help them view themselves and their peers as writers… To find joy in writing, even. Too good to be true? Not at all. The focus of my other two books is exactly this. It *is* possible to change perceptions about writing and writing competencies with our students. I've seen it happen time and again.

Writing Makes Us Vulnerable

If someone asked you—right now—to write something that will be sent home to your parent community in an hour, how would you feel? For most, there would be emotion attached to this, such as expectations (self-imposed or otherwise) and an inherent anxiety or pressure. Our writing reveals much about us: our capabilities, our weaknesses, our beliefs, our perspectives. Our students feel this, too. When you add the reality that they are *beginning* writers, that the process itself still requires much deliberate thought and attention, we can see why writing is intimidating for many students. And if writing itself brings about expectation and emotion, then the sharing of our writing does even more so.

Writing is risk-taking. Once again, it becomes clear why our teachers must establish positive relationships with their students. As Bright (2021) says, "Positive relationships build trust, psychological safety, and motivation" (19). These three—trust, psychological safety, and motivation—are all critical if we are going to motivate our students to write and write well. In fact, these factors are critical within our staffs as well. Being asked to present to their colleagues can be intimidating for some of our teachers; it is certainly easier if trust and safety have been established. Even when I am a guest in a classroom for a writing residency (someone about to ask students to write), I must find ways to connect with students and develop some sense of trust in an exceptionally short time.

The vulnerability students feel about writing is real. I've asked many students over the years what they don't like about writing or what they find difficult. And no matter the age of the students, the answers are always similar. Many will say

Understanding our students' reluctance to write helps us, as administrators, understand some of our teachers' hesitation and struggle to teach writing to their students.

some version of "I can't spell." Others will express the vulnerability through statements like "I'm not a good writer" or "I don't want anyone to read what I write." As an educator yourself, I'm sure you've asked your students to write and heard the refrain, "I don't know what to write." This is true whether we teach Grade 1 or Grade 12 or anywhere in between. It's funny that many of our students have so much to say, and yet when we ask them to write they're paralyzed.

In this chapter, I will explain the practices I put in place to address the concerns shared by many students. Keep in mind that many of the skills we've addressed in previous chapters assist our students with writing. For example, if we use oral language to our advantage, we can support students in generating ideas for their writing. If they feel confident with phonemic awareness, sight words, and using the word wall, we can limit some of their insecurities about spelling. Once again, the strands of language reveal how interconnected they are.

Daily Writing Practice

Our students should be writing daily. In Chapter 2, I introduced the idea of low-stakes writing as a way for our students to engage in their learning throughout the day, regardless of the curricular topic. In addition to helping them engage in their learning, this writing is also writing practice. If you look back at the weekly language-arts schedules on page 33, you'll notice that I embedded different forms of writing within the week: journal writing, freewriting, and reader response. These are not the only forms of writing our students will engage in throughout the year, but they are the forms students will use on a regular basis. Teachers will also ask students to write narratives, many forms of nonfiction text, and poetry.

Natalie Goldberg (2014) has said this about writing: "Like running, the more you do it, the better you get at it" (11). Do the students in your school write daily?

Although our students should be writing *something* daily, this writing is not limited to the confines of language arts. Some of the writing will occur within other subject areas as well, and not all of it will need to be graded or shared.

Emergent Writers

How do we support our beginning writers? How do our Grade 1 teachers do it?

Phonological awareness, phonemic awareness, and orthographic mapping are all going to provide our students with the foundational skills to begin writing. Sentence starters are also incredibly useful for these students. For example, perhaps we have recently orthographically mapped the word *like*. Our writing that day might begin with the prompt *I like…*. I would expect students to write these two words with conventional spelling. If a student completes the sentence with "chocolate ice cream," I would not expect those words to be spelled correctly; however, I would expect to see some reasonable attempts based on the student's letter-sound knowledge. This is known as *invented spelling* and is a critical step for our emergent writers. They are beginning to find the confidence to take risks and use their knowledge to communicate through writing.

The next time you are in a Grade 1 or 2 classroom, ask to look at the students' writing notebooks. What do you notice? Are students using invented spelling for more challenging words?

Grade 1 teachers, in particular, must be incredibly careful not to over-correct their students' attempts. Too much correction tends to stifle our students and can affect their willingness to take risks. Instead, we continue to focus on the phonemic awareness and orthographic mapping that scaffold our students for future writing. We honor their attempts as they learn this enormous new skill.

Learning to Write in Various Forms

Although you, as the administrator, will likely not teach writing to students, it is helpful to understand the types of writing that will occur in your elementary classrooms and the rationale for each. As previously discussed, teachers should embed writing into their weekly schedules. Their long-range plans will also reveal a focus on particular genres throughout the year. The types of writing most frequently being done in elementary schools are freewriting, journal writing, reader response, narrative writing, nonfiction writing, and poetry. As this section will explain, they each serve different a purpose for our elementary-age students.

Freewriting

"Freewriting is the easiest way to get words on paper and the best all-around practice in writing that I know." (Elbow 1998, 13)

I have always enjoyed writing. So much so that I went into a local journalism program out of high school. But the profession was not the right fit for me. When I shifted gears and went into education, I knew that was the place I was meant to be. But writing never left me. About the time I began teaching Grade 6, I was also diving back into my own writing more seriously and I noticed how reluctant many of my students were to write. When I discovered *freewriting*—a term coined by Peter Elbow—I decided to try it with my Grade 6 students.

Freewriting is sometimes misunderstood by both teachers and administrators and thought to be an extra, even fluff. And yet, as you will see, it is a transformative process. In my experience, the schools that have had the most success improving student writing embrace freewriting on a school-wide level.

It is not hyperbolic to say that bringing freewriting into my classroom changed my career, and hopefully the lives of many students along the way. When I first introduced freewriting to my Grade 6 students, I didn't expect it to have such immediate impact. Students were writing willingly, even joyfully! This writing approach also affected every other form of writing in my class. Then, as I shared freewriting with other classes and other teachers, I realized the power and promise it held in our elementary classrooms to significantly change student views toward writing. Colleagues began asking how to bring freewriting into their classrooms, which led to school-wide professional development. This led to division-wide professional development and my eventual shift into the role of language-arts consultant. These collective experiences prompted me to write teacher resources and provide in-services to teachers on this topic. It also grounds the writing residencies I do with students.

So… what is freewriting?

Freewriting refers to a process of continuous writing: it is a short, timed writing session where we keep our pens or pencils moving across the paper. During the freewrite, we are not concerned with spelling or grammar, punctuation or capitalization. We don't ignore them, but they are not our focus at this time. I agree that proper conventions in writing are important. However, the process of freewriting is just that, a process. Not worrying about conventions, including spelling, during the actual writing is liberating for students, and removes one of the stumbling blocks they themselves have identified.

Overthinking about the end product is a common problem with our elementary-level writers. Elbow (1998) speaks about writers more generally: "Sometimes, in fact, when people think too much during the early stages about what they want to end up with, that preoccupation with the final product keeps them from attaining it." (7)

When I first read about freewriting for adults, I noticed that there was not necessarily a prompt to guide the writing. This is one part of the process for which I made adaptations for students. I find that when students are given a short two- or three-word prompt and asked to write the first thing that comes to mind—without censoring their thoughts, without worrying about someone reading their work—they begin writing. I tell them to continue with that thought until they no longer have anything else to say about that topic. If their brain stops and, therefore, their hand stops, they rewrite the prompt and then again write the first thing that comes to mind. They continue this way until the time has elapsed.

Prompts do not have to be complicated. It is surprising where prompts such as *I remember…, I am…, I need…,* or *I wish my parents knew…* can lead!

How long do we engage in this continuous writing? Initially I strive for about six or seven minutes. Although it is not a long period of time, it is surprising how much our students can write when they are writing continuously. This short amount of time is reasonable for students of all grade levels. (I begin freewriting as early as January in Grade 1. From that point on, it is effective with everyone, including adults!) Consider our youngest writers: it takes them longer to physically print the words and also use their new-found phonetic knowledge. Six or seven minutes is ideal for them. Consider our older writers: because the actual process is faster, they can write quite a lot during this time. In fact, the students are often surprised at the amount they write during this short time.

Is it all brilliant, profound writing? Mine sure isn't. But freewriting—especially at the beginning—is about the process. It helps us break down barriers in our minds and changes our expectation of writing something perfectly the first time. The process is liberating for students. In fact, they are often impressed with their own writing when the internal censor or desire to impress has been lifted. As Goldberg (2005) says in *Writing Down the Bones*:

> …the aim is to burn through to first thoughts, to the place where energy is unobstructed by social politeness or the internal censor, to the place where you are writing what your mind actually sees and feels, not what it *thinks* it should see or feel. (8–9)

It works—for adults and for students.

Another aspect of freewriting that contributes to it being low-stakes—and is critical for classroom success—is giving students the choice of whether or not to share what they've written on a particular day. The knowledge of this choice significantly influences the writing. It allows students to write more freely because they aren't thinking, "My teacher is going to read this." They know they will have the choice. Another surprise for me when I introduced this process: my students were proud of what they had written and started to share more willingly, even those students who had been the most reluctant.

Once this process is established and we are writing regularly, students accumulate quite a body of writing. This body of work becomes useful as I teach specific mini-lessons on how to write well. Freewriting gets words on paper; there is so much we can do with those words. The process of writing—including revision and editing—becomes much clearer to students. (We will explore this further when we dive into the specifics of the writing process within our classrooms.)

One last important point about freewriting: I encourage teachers to write with students during this time. Students are more willing to engage in the process when they see their teacher doing the same and they realize that they cannot ask questions during the freewrite (a popular avoidance strategy when they don't want to write). Perhaps more importantly, the teacher learns a lot about the process when they engage in freewriting with their students. Those teachers who once said they are not writers themselves become writers alongside their students.

I once had a teacher call me back into her classroom saying that freewriting just wasn't working; students were not as engaged in the process as they were when I introduced it to her class. When I went back and observed, the problem became clear immediately. The teacher was not writing with her students; in fact, she was looking over shoulders and reading what they were writing as they were

Eventually I increase the time of the freewrite as students are ready. Typically, though, even when students are comfortable with the process, I try to stay under ten minutes so that all students feel successful.

When principals recognize the power of this practice throughout the school, it becomes embedded into the writing culture. I have witnessed a number of incredible administrators who have come into classrooms to engage in the process of freewriting with their students, demonstrating how much they value this type of writing.

writing. Tension in the room was high and the premise and power of freewriting was lost. The teachers who find freewriting most successful are the ones experiencing the process alongside their students.

There is no need for teachers to write narrative stories, journal entries, or nonfiction text alongside their students, except as a shared writing experience. But engaging in the process of freewriting with students makes for powerful learning for all.

Journal Writing

Do the students in your school write regularly in journals? Is it embedded into your teachers' weekly schedules?

My weekly schedule for language arts includes journal writing first thing Monday morning. This time is effective because it enables me to connect with each student at the beginning of the week. When they arrive in class on Mondays, students find their journals on their desks with a short comment or question from me. They are excited to see what I have written to them. The other reason Mondays are effective is because our elementary students (unlike older students, perhaps) have much to tell us, after a weekend especially. I'd like to listen to each of them tell me what happened to their cat or who won the soccer game, but I can't possibly listen to all of them as immediately as they want to tell me. But through writing? Yes!

After students hand in their journals, I have the entire week to read them and write a short response to each of them. This private writing connects me to my students in a way that isn't always possible otherwise.

One important note about journals: I never correct my students' journal writing for spelling, punctuation, or grammar. Ever. Journals are meant as a way of connecting us and is another form of writing practice. When journals are "marked up" by the teacher, students do not feel the content was valued; all they see is that the teacher found mistakes. These students become less motivated to write. I expect my students to ensure the word-wall words are spelled correctly for any piece of writing they hand in, including their journals (see page 58). I encourage them to put into practice their phonemic knowledge and the words we have been orthographically mapping. But if I notice mistakes, journals are not the place to point them out.

There is one slight difference in the journal-writing process for Grades 1 and 2. I ask these students to put their hands up when they are finished writing and then to read the journal to me. This routine helps students get into the habit of reading over their work; it also gives me an opportunity to hear what they have attempted to write. In addition to possibly helping me decipher their invented spelling, I can also check for conventional spelling of word-wall words and for punctuation. If a student has spelled a word-wall word incorrectly, I can remind them to look back to the wall and make the change. If they have forgotten to use punctuation, I can remind them. I'm not marking up their pages, but I am giving the guidance they need at this stage. As I tell Grade 1 and 2 teachers, this is perhaps the most important part of journal writing for these emerging writers, as they can be provided immediate, differentiated support.

Reader Response

We know that reading and writing are flip sides of the same coin. Reader-response writing provides a wonderful way for students to engage with text. If teachers involve students in a class discussion about a book, only the same three or four students tend to respond. However, if we give everyone the chance to write, all students can engage more deeply in the text. Madeleine L'Engle has said, "Stories make us more alive, more human, more courageous, more loving." Books are the springboard and the writing provides time to reflect and connect, ultimately helping students think beyond their own experience. In her book *Unselfie,* Michele Borba (2016) cites research that indicates, "people who read fiction are more capable of understanding others, empathizing and seeing another person's point of view than those who read nonfiction" (78–79). Reader-response writing, then, is not only another form of writing practice, it also helps our students navigate their world.

Because I teach all grades to freewrite, when we begin reader-response writing, students understand that this writing is also low-stakes writing. They are more willing to write and, in fact, many students write continuously as they would a freewrite. To make the process as easy as possible, I give them prompts, as I would in freewriting. Often, though, there are a few prompts to choose from to ensure all students can connect to the text we have read. For example, if I have read the picture book *A Family Is a Family Is a Family* to my students, I would put three prompts on the board for students to choose from: *I noticed…, My family…,* and *Families….* Students might stay with one prompt the whole time, but they have the option of moving from one to another if they choose. I always try to use at least one prompt that focuses on the book itself and then another that focuses on the reader's reaction or connection to the book.

Beers and Probst (2017) introduced the Book, Head, Heart (BHH) framework as a type of reader response. I appreciate that this framework begins with a short summary of what has been read (*what's in the book*), and then provides students with the opportunity to share both what they are thinking (*what's in my head*) and what they are feeling (*what's in my heart*). Because I find the use of short sentence starters as prompts so powerful, I use them within this framework as well: for example, *In this book…, I am thinking…,* and *I feel….*

Do you ever share a book with students at an assembly or on broadcast? At a Thanksgiving celebration, for example, I would sometimes read a book such as *The Grateful Book* by Angela Kohler, *Thankful* by Eileen Spinelli, or *Last Stop on Market Street* by Matt De La Pena. Students of all grades would return to their classrooms to engage in a reader response: *I am thankful for….* As administrators, we can be an example to both students and teachers, valuing writing as a means of thought and reflection.

Once students are familiar with simple reader-response prompts, perhaps you can introduce the Book, Head, Heart framework at a staff meeting. Teachers could adapt the experience for the grade level they teach and introduce the strategy to their students. Then, after a subsequent assembly, everyone in the school could use this framework to respond to a shared text.

I recommend reader-response writing once a week in our elementary classrooms. I begin this process as early as Kindergarten! These students can certainly respond to text through pictures, and, in time, some will even begin to add writing to the page. Administrators, and even teachers, are sometimes surprised that curricula across the country embed personal reactions to text in their outcomes. In Nova Scotia, for example, one of the outcomes in the Language

Arts Curriculum is: *Learners will respond personally and critically to a range of culturally diverse texts.* The indicators under this outcome for primary students (Kindergarten) include drawing pictures (or pictures with labels and/or text) about their personal reactions. In the older grades, the expected responses become more complex. Reader-response writing, then, should not be viewed as an extra, but rather as a meaningful way to meet curricular outcomes.

Narrative Writing

Narrative writing is common in elementary classrooms. Students are reading narratives frequently at this point and this is a wonderful entry point into mini-lessons on writing. We can read and enjoy a good story, yes. But then… oh, the magic that happens when we dive in and examine the craft of the writer! And because I call my students "writers" and they begin to view themselves as such, they realize that they, too, can make these craft decisions in their own writing.

Narratives engage young students. Most students, when choosing what to read, choose some form of narrative story. We can capitalize on their interest in stories to help them become more confident, competent writers. School-wide writing experiences commonly use narratives; they will be discussed later in the chapter (see page 95).

As an administrator, any actions you take to help create and support a culture where written forms of communication are encouraged and celebrated are most welcome!

Nonfiction

When we consider the language demands placed on our students in this ever-changing world, we realize that they are expected to read a wide variety of texts for a wide variety of purposes. Think about the number of times a day students are asked to read instructions—on assignments, on tests, on experiments, etc.—and, in fact, how the frequency of these situations will only increase as they move up the grade levels. They also read extensive nonfiction text in the content areas—think of the variety of reading material in science, social studies, and mathematics. And again, the frequency of this text will increase with each passing grade level. If you consider the content of your own reading material, I would anticipate the majority of your day-to-day reading would be nonfiction: documents, instructions, manuals, signs, recipes, and reports, just to name a few.

Writing nonfiction text in school can take many forms. Perhaps the most common are reports, recipes, instructions, autobiographies, and letters. It is often when students try to write a particular form of text that they understand the elements and purpose of that text more completely. There are features, processes, and sometimes protocols involved in writing nonfiction that are not as prevalent in fiction. For example, in nonfiction text, the inclusion of diagrams and text features is quite common. Research is often a necessary process when writing reports or informational text. Sequencing and clarity are also essential. The writing of a recipe might seem like an odd thing to teach our students to do, yet the process is powerful. Students must list ingredients (one form of writing, in fact) and then write a sequence of steps (another form of writing). If their writing is not sequential or clear to the reader, the recipe will not work. During my lessons on writing recipes, students come to understand the importance of reading over their work and the need for revision. I remember a Grade 2 student who, after reading me the draft of her recipe, exclaimed, "That doesn't make sense. I have to change the order of those steps!" She was a sincere writer (and reviser) at work.

One of the most significant differences between the types of writing is purpose. Journals are designed to be a reflective process and sometimes a personal exchange between two people. Narratives are usually meant to engage and entertain. Nonfiction text is typically meant to inform, instruct, explain, persuade, or retell. The purpose changes the nature of our writing. Do you see students writing in various forms within your school?

Poetry

Language-arts curricula throughout the country include poetry. Our students should be exposed to poetry and reading poetry throughout the year. As discussed in earlier chapters, poetry can be a wonderful way to engage students in shared reading: as a way to practice fluency, as a reason for repeated readings, and as a source of enjoyment for students, who tend to appreciate the playfulness of poetry. Although the reading of poetry occurs throughout the year, the writing of poetry is usually more limited. Some curricula are specific about which types of poems students should be reading and writing at which grade levels. In other places, it is more open-ended.

Teachers will often expose their students to a type of poem and then engage in shared writing, writing one together, before students are asked to write one themselves. This is a way to scaffold the process and ensure students are familiar with the structure. Elementary students and teachers often enjoy manipulating language and playing with words to create poems!

As an administrator, I created a *poetry walk* within the school. Each student would choose their favorite poem among those they had written and create a polished version to be put on the bulletin board outside their classroom. Then, on a particular afternoon, we would play music in the hallways as students walked around the school, reading the poetry. To ensure it didn't get too crowded around the bulletin boards, we would schedule a few classes at a time. Sending students around the school with their reading buddies was an effective way of ensuring that all students could read or hear the poetry written by their classmates.

The Writing Process at Work in Our Classrooms

Many teachers have shared that they feel less confident teaching writing than they do teaching reading. The skill of writing is broad and involves an overwhelming number of components (a quick glance at a writing rubric confirms this). When teaching our students to improve their writing, we must find ways to make it manageable.

In *Freewriting with Purpose*, I included this diagram to help guide teachers in the process of teaching writing. I also use it during most of the professional development I provide.

The writing process is not intuitive for all teachers. Sharing this diagram and talking about it as a staff can be useful. The discussion could help teachers answer the question referred to on page 81: *Do you assign written tasks to your students or do you teach your students how to write?*

A Structure for Teaching Skills

- Determine which skill to teach
- Choose mentor texts
- Teach the mini-lesson
- Students revise their chosen freewrites
- Students discuss writing in writing groups
- Students continue to revise

Sometimes...

Edit & Publish/Assess

This structure can guide teachers for any skill and in any genre they are teaching. It is a process that will be repeated time and again. Everything you see to the right of the diagonal line is what teachers should be doing; everything to the left of the line is what we guide our students to do. This structure capitalizes on the gradual release of responsibility. Let's walk through the elements.

Determine Which Skill to Teach

The first step for teachers is determining which specific skill they want to teach. Many teachers have shared that they don't know where to look for the skills to teach within writing lessons. I direct them to use a specific curricular outcome (e.g., *Include a range of sentence beginnings and types to vary and add interest to writing*) or a specific area of their writing rubric. The example outcome listed here is exactly what you would find on a rubric under *sentence fluency*. Therefore, using either of these sources to determine the skill to teach—curricular outcomes or the rubric—will ultimately help teachers decide on a topic for their mini-lesson.

Mentor Texts and Mini-Lessons

As you read about this process, it becomes clear why elementary teachers prefer a longer language-arts block within their timetables. In my experience, most elementary teachers schedule language arts in the morning. Ensuring that all classes have some days with an extended block of morning instruction not interrupted by music or physical education is important.

Referring back to the diagram, you see that, once teachers have decided on a specific skill to teach, they can choose mentor texts for their mini-lesson. In Chapter 3, I mentioned the need for mentor texts. It is during our mini-lessons on writing that mentor texts become essential. Mentor texts provide us with an opportunity to study the author's craft. As Routman (2014) says, "We can't teach a first-rate lesson with second-rate texts" (97). Whatever skill we are learning, in whatever genre, we must read and analyze mentor texts.

A natural by-product of using mentor texts is that our students become more effective and capable readers. Why? Remember the Systems of Strategic Action (see page 68)—Thinking Within, Beyond, and About the Text. The two subskills in Thinking About the Text are analyzing and critiquing. This occurs as we study mentor texts before we write. So although the mini-lesson is geared to writing, our students gain information and insight that they use when they are reading other texts of that genre, too, and ultimately improve their comprehension.

Choose Freewrite and Begin Revising

The next part of the diagram is where we release some of the responsibility to our students: we move from the explicit teaching (*I do*) to the guided instruction (*We do*). As part of our mini-lesson, after we have examined various mentor texts, I invite the students to revisit their freewrite and begin the process of revision.

Since our students are freewriting regularly, they have a growing body of writing. Before my mini-lesson, I ask students to choose one of their favorite freewrites. If we are working on improving such skills as adding details to our work, sentence fluency, or word choice, we can typically use any type of writing; therefore, our freewriting is ideal. If we are teaching a skill specific to a genre, such as character development in narrative writing or adding text features to our nonfiction writing, we would have students use a draft from that genre.

> A breakthrough I had as a teacher was to have students use previously written work for mini-lessons. Instead of teaching them a particular skill and asking them to write new content while using that skill, I realized that I could reduce their cognitive load. When students use a freewrite of their choosing (or other previously written text), they do not have to generate new content but can instead focus on the skill I am teaching. Sounds simple, and yet it transformed my teaching and empowered my students.

One of the most common complaints I hear teachers make about their students' writing is about students' reluctance to revise. In many classrooms, after writing, students will exclaim "I'm done!" and, truly, they think they are. The idea of a growth mindset in the writing process is essential. If students believe that their work is "good enough," then why would they revise?

How do we change this? It's all in our approach. I embed the process of revision into our mini-lessons. If we have studied several mentor texts and realized the deliberate word choices used by the authors (e.g., alliteration or interesting verbs), when we send students back to their own writing, they have something specific to revise.

Perhaps students think they are "done" because of the way we have conditioned them to write. But when they begin to understand writing as a process—when we examine mentor texts together and talk about the author's craft, when they see ways to improve their work, and we guide them through the process of revision—they are empowered to make changes, and they do!

Writing Groups

Moving through the diagram, you'll notice that, after the initial revision, I ask students to meet with their writing groups. These are pre-established groups that my students become quite accustomed to. Peer feedback can be powerful in our elementary classrooms. I remember standing next to a Grade 1 teacher as her

The terms *revision* and *editing* are often used interchangeably in classrooms. The easiest way to distinguish between the two for teachers and students is to think of our rubric. Revision typically deals with all of the elements of our rubric *except* conventions, those big decisions we make about our writing. Editing (for students) typically focuses on conventions, fine-tuning the details to make our work both readable and presentable.

students gave feedback to each other during writing groups. She was astounded at what her students were saying, how they were saying it, and how receptive the writer was to this feedback. Of course, I had scaffolded the experience for them and taught them how to give appropriate feedback to each other (using language from my mini-lesson). Even so, the level of feedback would surprise most teachers.

Revision After Writing Groups

If we truly want the feedback given during writing groups to be used, we must give students time after their writing groups to continue with their revision. It does not have to be much time, but a few minutes for writers to continue making changes based on feedback places value on the feedback itself.

Editing

You'll notice on the diagram that editing (as well as publishing and assessment) are in the centre with a caveat: *Sometimes.* There is no need for students to take every piece of writing to the final stage or for teachers to assess everything they write. In fact, both of these practices stifle young writers. If you notice that not all student writing is edited, this may be why. Understanding the rationale behind this practice is also helpful when talking to parents.

My general guideline is this: Whenever my students are handing in a piece of writing—a journal entry, a narrative story, a nonfiction report on light and sound—I expect them to edit their work. In fact, I scaffold the process for them. They are reminded to use the word wall, their phonemic knowledge, and their sight-word vocabulary. I also give them time to read their writing out loud, which is often when they catch errors.

When marking their students' writing, it is important for teachers to remember that conventions make up only one section of the rubric. A student with poor conventions could quite possibly be a strong writer in all other areas. A lack of conventions can be deceiving. That being said, we know that conventions—or the lack of them—make a first impression. Proper conventions make our writing easier to read. If my work is riddled with errors, the validity of what I am saying is lost. Readers might question my message: either I don't know enough to understand the conventions of language, or I don't care enough about you, the reader, to use them.

The Importance of Feedback

Working through the writing process should include regular feedback. For myself, as a writer, feedback is a critical opportunity to push both my thinking and my writing. I recognize that without it, my writing would not be as strong. The same is true for our students. The idea of feedback is dependent on sharing our work. Because of this, I try to give my students choice in what they share whenever possible.

First, let's consider what *not* to do when giving feedback. I've alluded to some of this already. We do not want to take our red pen and mark up our elementary students' writing. This can be defeating for our young writers. Consider it from a young writer's perspective: *I've taken a risk, put my ideas on paper, tried to*

Could this guideline become something you discuss as a staff? If all teachers approached editing in this way, with an explicit expectation for students to edit whatever it is they are handing in, it could lead to more consistency and understanding throughout the school.

If you find yourself evaluating a teacher on a language-arts lesson on writing, understanding the pedagogy behind writing instruction, feedback, and assessment is advantageous.

remember all there is to know about this business called writing, but all the teacher sees are my errors. Over time, a student starts to believe: *I'm not a good writer. I don't like writing. Why should I bother trying when all I do is make mistakes?*

I have seen teachers of all grade levels mark up their students' pages. This is done with good intentions, of course. The teacher is pointing out where and how students could improve. Yet how many students take the time to figure out what changes have been suggested, let alone carry them forward to their next piece of writing? John Almarode and Kara Vandas (2019) put it this way: "By sheer volume, this feedback paralyzes a learner as to what to do in response" (139). Students who receive this type of feedback are likely too distracted by the emotion of the experience to make any changes to their work. Besides, this practice does not fit into the gradual release of responsibility we have come to understand is so important with our young students: correcting their mistakes *for* them will not lead to transfer.

At the other extreme, perhaps less common in elementary classrooms, is the teacher simply putting at grade at the top of the page. No comments, no feedback, just a letter or number. I experienced this as a student and found it incredibly frustrating. I had no idea what I was doing to get that grade or what I could do to improve.

Let's find some middle ground. What should teachers be doing to provide feedback to our elementary students?

Forms of Teacher Feedback

Feedback from teachers can come in many forms: oral comments, written comments, references to a portion of the rubric, and the use of single-point rubrics. When you are visiting classrooms in your school, watch for feedback in these forms.

Oral Feedback

When we consider all that goes into the effective teaching of writing, it becomes clear why some teachers feel overwhelmed.

Although teachers freewrite with their students, for other forms of writing, such as narratives or nonfiction, I encourage teachers to circulate, engage in a quick conference with an individual student, and provide immediate feedback. Rather than notice a problem area when the writing is submitted—and therefore lose the timely, teachable moment—teachers can circulate and support students as they engage in the writing process, providing timely oral feedback. This time spent circulating is time spent differentiating. How? Timely, individual feedback enables us to ensure the skills we have taught are being attempted, support those writers who struggle, and push those who excel.

Feedback can be given both by the teacher and by peers. Just as we must practice giving effective feedback, considering the tone and our intent, the same is true for our students. Giving quality feedback is a skill to be developed by administrator, teacher, and student alike.

Short writing conferences with students can also be scheduled. If I plan to conference with three students the next day, I put a sticky note on the three students' desks, letting them know about the upcoming conference. The note gives them time to think about what they want to talk about and it also holds me accountable for the meeting. The conferences do not have to be long, but they are a chance to touch base with our writers.

Written Comments

As you can see, sticky notes are used for many purposes in elementary classrooms. Providing your teachers with a generous supply can be a fun (yet practical) surprise!

Many teachers like to give written comments to their writers so that students can go back and reread them. Whether they are written directly on the student's writing, on a sticky note attached to the writing, or using the Comments feature in a digital format, comments lets teachers provide specific feedback to each student. One caution: less is more.

Using a Portion of the Rubric

If my mini-lesson is on, say, word choice, as I referred to earlier, perhaps I isolate that section of the rubric. I do not have to assess the writing in all areas, but I can look specifically at the student's word choice and mark the rubric accordingly. I would also add a short, written comment. Typically, this feedback would be intended as formative assessment (feedback given during the process to help students improve) rather than summative assessment (feedback used to evaluate student progress at the completion of an assignment).

Single-Point Rubrics

Giving teachers time to collaborate on the creation of single-point rubrics is something to consider within your school. The discussion that surrounds the creation of rubrics—any type of rubric—is powerful professional learning.

Over the past few years, I have started using single-point rubrics more regularly. They accomplish the same function as isolating a part of the rubric, but are often more user-friendly for students. I can also tailor the rubrics with the precise language used in my mini-lessons for any topic: dialogue, character development, sentence fluency, text features, anything! These rubrics can be used for teacher feedback, peer feedback, or even self-reflection.

The precise focus of my mini-lesson becomes evident when reading the criteria column of the single-point rubric shown below. These rubrics can guide students when they look at their own work. After reading their own writing, they can note where they see room for improvement (*GROW*). And they can comment on what they are doing well (*GLOW*)—even jotting down specific words that apply to the criteria.

Word Choice		
GROW	**CRITERIA** for proficient performance/product	**GLOW**
	I can **find** interesting words used by an author.	
	I can **use specific** and **interesting** words in my writing.	
	I can **use descriptive words** to paint a picture in the reader's mind.	

Effective Feedback Should Be...

Regardless of the form of the feedback given by teachers, there are consistent qualities of effective feedback. To help our students improve their writing, feedback should be timely, targeted, and actionable. As you read through these sections, consider how you might model effective feedback with your staff.

Timely

Feedback should be timely in a few ways. Consider this: have you ever handed in something to a teacher and by the time you received it back, you had forgotten what you had written? The further away the feedback is from the time of writing, the less effective it is.

Feedback should also be given throughout the process of learning and not only at the completion of an assignment. If we are treating feedback as something to learn from (i.e., as formative assessment), why give it at the end without students having the opportunity to use it to improve their work? Unfortunately, this is a common misstep in our classrooms, one that I made for many years. Thankfully, it is easily rectified.

Targeted

It is not effective to say to our elementary students, "Revise your writing." Students truly do not understand what we mean by this and it's no wonder teachers become frustrated when students stare blankly at their pages. Students must understand both *what* and *how* to revise their writing. I encourage teachers to use the language from their mini-lessons to help guide students with revision. For example, if the class has been exploring mentor texts and analyzing the writer's craft in regards to the organization of ideas, this gives us something specific on which to provide feedback.

Teachers should provide both positive and constructive feedback. When giving positive feedback, it is important to avoid general comments that don't help students understand what they did well. Compared with saying, "Good work," you will find a starter like "I like the way you…" much more effective. This ensures students understand specifically what they are doing well.

It is also important to give students constructive feedback so they can improve their work. Focusing on one or two areas based on pre-established criteria will be most effective. Too much feedback at once can easily overwhelm our young students.

Actionable

The third quality of effective feedback is that it is actionable. Students should have an authentic opportunity to use the feedback, which is why we don't reserve feedback for the end of the process. Our feedback should inspire and enable our students to make changes to their work; this is revision, after all. Giving actionable feedback does not mean that we have to provide the answers. Questions to help students think more deeply about their work are actionable as well: e.g., "Have you considered…?" When teacher feedback is done well, most students welcome it, as it provides direction in how to improve their work.

Writing Assessments

Much of our students' writing in elementary classrooms should be low-stakes with no formal assessment attached. This allows for regular writing practice. Assessing everything our students write accomplishes two of the wrong things:

1. students become (or remain) reluctant to write, feeling the pressure of assessment

"By being constructive, effective feedback serves a very useful purpose: learning." (Almarode and Vandas 2019, 136)

A teacher's workload is demanding and ever-evolving. Acknowledging and reminding teachers that assessment is not required on all student writing will gain you great respect as an administrator.

2. teachers don't ask their students to write as frequently because they believe they have to assess everything being written

How often should teachers assess their students' writing? I formally assess writing sparingly. Assessment is important, yes. But more important is the work leading up to the assessment. Assessment occurs only when our students have had the opportunity to take their writing through the writing process. I would never assess a raw piece of student writing. Just as I wouldn't want someone to assess my work-in-progress or my freewriting, students need the opportunity to revise and edit their work when they know they are preparing it for assessment.

Rubrics

Rubrics are the most common tool to assess writing. The benefit of rubrics is that they break the assessment into various components. In elementary schools, you will often hear about the 6 + 1 Traits of Writing (ideas and content, organization, voice, word choice, sentence fluency, and conventions, with presentation being the +1). The rubrics based on these traits can be used for many genres of writing.

If you have multiple teachers teaching the same grade, it can be effective for them to agree on the use of one rubric. I also encourage teachers to assess their students' writing collaboratively every so often to ensure their standards are similar. By referring to common rubrics, teachers will use consistent language. When the rubrics are referred to regularly with students, students learn this language too.

Teachers can determine the focus of their mini-lessons through the language on their rubrics. By doing so, they are truly beginning with the end in mind! However, this might not be a strategy all teachers are familiar with.

School-Wide Writing Experiences

Many schools coordinate school-wide writing experiences, which may be referred to as a Write-On or as School-Wide Writes. Sometimes these school-wide writing experiences connect with writing that students are expected to do on provincial exams. In Alberta, for example, Grade 6 students write an exam in May that requires both a narrative story and a news article. To support students with these tasks, many schools organize school-wide narrative-writing experiences once or twice a year to facilitate teachers of all grades working toward the same end goal. The narrative form is usually chosen because it is something accessible to students at all grade levels.

There are many benefits to such an experience. When writing becomes a school-wide focus, we tend to use common language, we might develop common rubrics, and we could assess our students' work collaboratively. Students benefit because we are building on skills from year to year.

If you decide to organize a school-wide writing experience, be sure to involve teachers in the process and set aside time to mark collaboratively. It will be appreciated! Also, be sure to give teachers plenty of notice of the date and encourage them not to book anything else at this time. The experience is most valuable when everyone is present.

Scheduling School-Wide Writing

School-wide writing experiences can be scheduled at various times of the year, depending on the purpose. If we schedule a Write-On at the beginning of the year, it can become a wonderful starting point for our teachers' writing instruction. After they collaboratively assess their students' narratives, they will have a better idea of their current abilities and also which skills to target during instruction. Some skills will be specific to narratives, such as plot, character development, setting, and dialogue. Some of the skills will apply to many genres of writing—all of the 6 + 1 traits of writing—and help improve our students' writing in any genre.

If we begin the year with a narrative Write-On, the teaching of narratives can occur throughout the year. Teachers will certainly shift to focus on other forms of writing, but returning to narratives periodically throughout the year is effective. Because I use **plot patterns** with students, each time I revisit narrative writing I introduce a new plot pattern to my students. Many schools have adopted this practice to help support teachers in teaching narratives to their students and to improve student understanding of story structure.

It can be effective to schedule a second Write-On near the end of the year so teachers and students have something specific to work toward. The comparison between the two Write-On's will reflect the growth that occurred during the year. This experience is not only good for teachers, but also for students, who are often surprised to see how their writing changed over the year.

In places with a provincial or regional achievement test, like Alberta, it is beneficial to schedule the school-wide writing for the same day. That way, all students in the school are writing and we can ensure a quiet learning environment for the experience, turning off bells and avoiding such disruptions as announcements or phone calls to the classroom. As an administrator, you set the tone for the experience.

For information on teaching narrative writing through plot patterns, refer to Chapter 6 in my book *How Do I Get Them to Write?* which explains the process in detail and provides graphic organizers for student use.

Choosing Picture Prompts

Knowing that the school-wide Write-On will be collaboratively assessed, it is most effective to choose a common picture prompt for everyone to use. Sometimes I choose a prompt for the entire school, sometimes I choose two, one for primary and one for upper elementary. Either way works.

When choosing prompts, it is best to use a picture that has at least one potential character for students to develop in their writing. An interesting setting is good, too, but including a person tends to encourage students to develop a character. I also look for an element of mystery within the prompts, something unknown or mysterious, or a quizzical expression on a person's face reacting to something not shown. Even with all of the resources on the internet, my favorite source of picture prompts are wordless picture books. This genre of books is ever-expanding. It is important that students do not see the whole book, which would give the image a particular context; rather, choose one picture to be used.

If you plan to use a picture prompt for a school-wide writing experience, be sure teachers know about it in advance. Perhaps you can ask teachers to submit possible prompts, or ask for volunteers to form a committee to do this. Involving staff in the process is often appreciated!

Another consideration when choosing prompts is background knowledge. If you have a diverse cultural population, strive to choose something that would spark an idea for most students.

Collaborative Marking

Knowing the time and concentration it takes to assess student writing, as an administrator I scheduled time for teachers to assess the school-wide writing collaboratively. If possible, collaborative marking might take the place of a regular staff meeting. If necessary, teachers can be given release time to work with their colleagues. Although this can be financially taxing, many teachers have shared that collaborative marking is one of the most effective professional learning opportunities they have experienced. It is worth the investment!

How do we facilitate collaborative marking? Teachers of the same grade level sit together. Each teacher chooses two or three pieces of writing from their class that will be commonly assessed by all teachers of that grade level. Teachers assess these pieces of writing independently first. Then, they share their rubrics/scores to determine the similarities and differences in their scores. I remind teachers that there will be some variation, as the process is somewhat subjective. However, by assessing and then discussing five or six common pieces of writing first, they are likely to be more consistent as they assess the writing of the rest of their class. I encourage teachers to continue assessing the rest of the writing in the same room so they can ask each other questions as they come up. If you are in a small school with one teacher per grade level, it can be effective to pair with a neighboring school. Teachers often enjoy the opportunity to collaborate with a grade-level colleague.

In addition to giving my teachers time, I would also supply treats to keep them motivated and enhance concentration!

Instructional Walk Considerations: Writing

After reading and thinking more about the teaching of writing, consider these questions on your next instructional walk:

- What forms of writing do you see in your school?
- If you ask students how they feel about writing, what do they say?
- Are mini-lessons and mentor texts (especially picture books) being used to teach specific writing strategies?
- Would you say that your teachers assign written tasks or are they teaching students how to write?
- What is the teacher doing while students are writing?
- How are teachers providing feedback to student writers?
- How will you support teachers in continuing their own personal learning to support student writing?
- Could you create a writing station within your school? A school mail station or story-writing station, for example?
- Have you considered a school-wide writing experience? How would you ensure buy-in from your teachers? How would you value the time it takes?
- Is there a local children's author that you could bring into the school to talk to students about their own writing process?

Talk Time: Writing

Take some time to read and think about this diagram and these questions before discussing them with your colleagues. Choose a specific topic about writing that is most timely for you, or discuss the set(s) of questions decided upon by your school team.

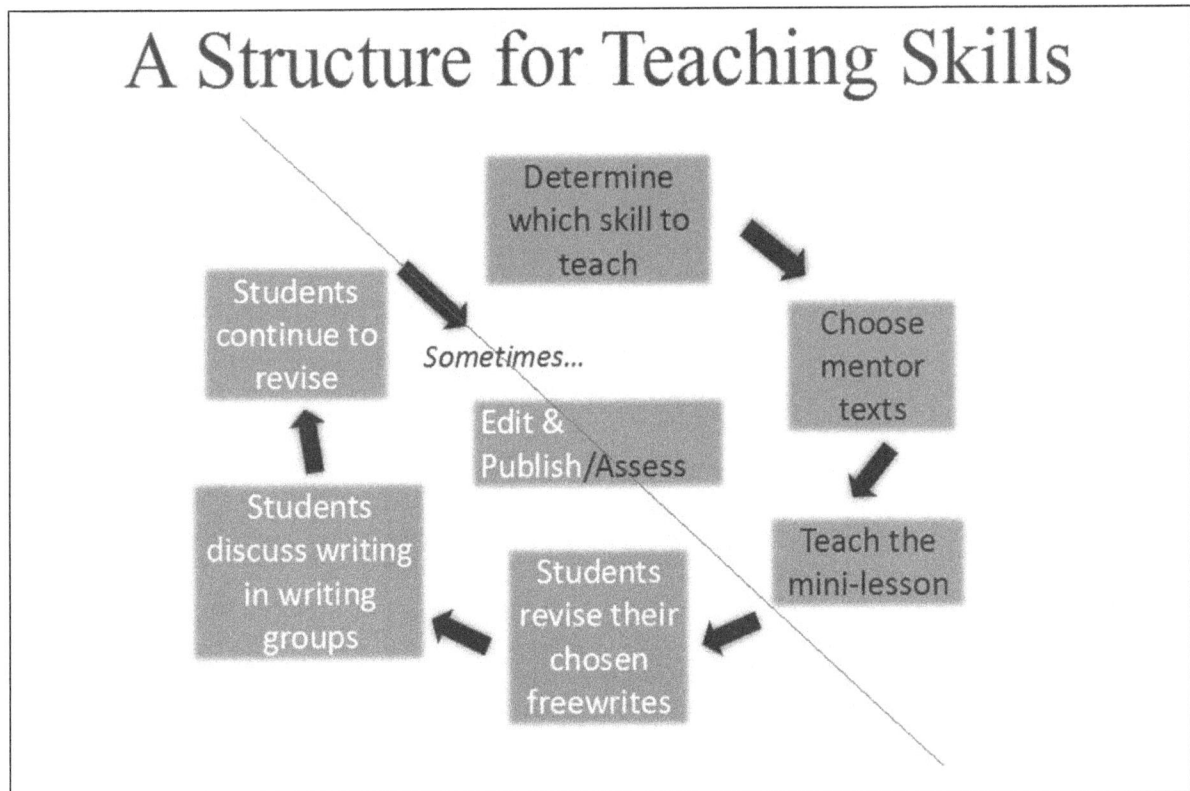

A Structure for Teaching Skills

- Determine which skill to teach
- Choose mentor texts
- Teach the mini-lesson
- Students revise their chosen freewrites
- Students discuss writing in writing groups
- Students continue to revise

Sometimes... Edit & Publish/Assess

The Writing Process

- What do you notice about this diagram? How is it similar to or different from the way you currently teach writing to your students?
- What do you find most challenging about the teaching of writing?
- Would you say that you assign written tasks to your students or do you teach them how to write? What's the difference?
- What specific writing strategies and skills do you teach your students? Have you considered referring to your rubric as a place to find your mini-lessons?
- Do you use mentor texts during your mini-lessons? What are your favorites for this purpose? Why?

Pembroke Publishers ©2023 *Literacy Leadership Matters* by Karen Filewych ISBN 978-1-55138-361-3

Talk Time: Writing (cont'd)

Freewriting

"Freewriting is the easiest way to get words on paper and the best all-around practice in writing that I know." (Elbow 1998, 13)

- What is your understanding of freewriting? Have you ever tried it with your students? What was your experience?
- What are you doing when your students are writing? How might you adjust your practice?

Feedback and Assessment

- How do you give feedback to your student writers? What do you find most effective? What do you find challenging about giving feedback?
- How often do you assess your student writing?
- Do you and your colleagues use a common rubric for writing assessment?

Pembroke Publishers ©2023 *Literacy Leadership Matters* by Karen Filewych ISBN 978-1-55138-361-3

8

Literacy in the Content Areas

"Reading is the gateway skill that makes all other learning possible."
— Barack Obama

The Power of Integration: Authenticity

Routman (2014) says, "More authenticity in tasks and content and in how we apply required curriculum and standards leads to more engagement and enjoyment, more motivated students, and higher comprehension." (165)

In elementary classrooms, most subjects are taught by the same teacher. This simple reality should affect our teachers' approach to planning and instruction. Integrating literacy into the content areas will have a positive impact on student learning, in both language arts and the other subject areas. In language arts, we learn to read and write. In the content areas, we read and write to help us learn and understand new material. Why not bring these two aims together, capitalizing on authentic opportunities to use the literacy skills we are learning throughout the day?

Do the teachers in your school intentionally integrate language learning into the other subject areas? If they're like me at the beginning of my teaching career, likely not. I now realize that I did not take advantage of opportunities to integrate. Instead, like those around me, I designed my schedule by separating the subjects into the required allotted minutes, and handed the timetable in to my administrator as requested. Then, throughout the year, I was constricted by the clock. At 1:30, I'd move on to science because that was what my schedule dictated. (Often my students would hold me accountable to the schedule, too!) Did I ever carry on with a lesson if we needed the time? Sometimes, but guilt would often accompany that extra time, since I wasn't adhering to the allotted minutes. I treated those subject areas in silos. Sure, my students were reading in science class, but it didn't occur to me to capitalize on that reading time to reinforce what we had learned that morning during language arts. It also did not occur to me to bring the text from science class into my language-arts lesson.

Of course, we must follow the curriculum and teach each subject area. I'm certainly not saying we should do away with timetables entirely but, particularly in elementary classrooms, we should consider how to capitalize on opportunities for integration, intentionally bringing literacy into the content areas and the content areas into language arts whenever possible. When your teachers are creating their timetables at the beginning of the year, engage in a discussion about integration. Perhaps this is an area that they want to improve upon. Perhaps it even becomes one of your school goals.

The Importance of Background Knowledge

One of my more recent understandings is the extent to which background knowledge factors into comprehension. I have always recognized that it plays some role. In fact, I often thought reading comprehension tests were unfair to recent immigrants, even those who speak English, given that their background knowledge is typically quite different from our own. Were they poor readers? Often not, but the tests sure didn't reveal that. Willingham (2017) concurs:

> We might think that reading tests provide an all-purpose measure of reading ability. But we've seen that reading comprehension depends heavily on how much the reader happens to know about the topic of the text. Perhaps then, reading comprehension tests are really knowledge tests in disguise. (127)

Sometimes my students seemed confident and competent as readers in language-arts class, then much less so in the content areas. This should point us to a few important factors: text type, vocabulary, content, and background knowledge. Willingham suggests,

> Teaching reading is not just a matter of teaching reading. The whole curriculum matters, because good readers have broad knowledge in civics, drama, history, geography, science the visual arts, and so on. (127)

If we return to the Simple View of Reading (see page 39), this makes sense.

Word Recognition × Language Comprehension = Reading Comprehension

Language comprehension includes both vocabulary and background knowledge. Even with comprehension strategies—such as visualization, connecting, or summarizing—in place, if I don't have background knowledge about a topic, my comprehension will remain limited.

There are a few examples circulating to prove this. In *Subjects Matter*, Harvey Daniels and Steven Zemelman (2014) provide this example of text:

> The Batsmen were merciless against the Bowlers. The Bowlers placed their men in slips and covers. But to no avail. The Batsmen hit one four after another along with an occasional six. Not once did their balls hit their stumps or get caught. (27)

To help teachers understand the role that background knowledge plays in comprehension, share the example provided by Daniels and Zemelman. Discuss how this idea relates to all students, especially the ELLs, within your school. Then consider: how do we ensure we are continually building background knowledge?

As you read this—unless you have the appropriate background knowledge—you may have found yourself somewhat confused and without full comprehension of the text. I suspect you did not have trouble decoding or recognizing any of the words. Yet until you know that this paragraph is about the game of cricket, it does not make a lot of sense. If you read it again now, knowing the topic, you might understand a little more than you did the first time through. But unless you have played or watched the game, there are likely still gaps in your comprehension, as there are for me. Through this example, the role of background knowledge in comprehension becomes clear.

In her book, *The Knowledge Gap*, Natalie Wexler (2019) says,

> While instruction in the early grades has focused on "learning to read" rather than "reading to learn," educators have overlooked the fact that part of "learning to read" is acquiring knowledge. (30)

Wexler acknowledges that the research points to decoding and word recognition as significant in learning to read. But when we consider comprehension and the teaching of skills, she says, "Teaching disconnected comprehension skills boosts neither comprehension nor reading scores" (29). Wexler, like Willingham, suggests grounding literacy instruction within authentic opportunities to read and write in the content areas. Integration should not be seen as a nice idea when we think of it. Teachers should intentionally integrate literacy into the content areas, understanding that it is a practice supported by research.

Enhancing Reading Comprehension Across the Curriculum

The instructional practices we use during language arts—read-alouds, shared reading, guided reading, partner reading, and independent reading—can support our teaching of content across the curriculum. Everything we learned about these instructional practices in Chapter 6 remains true when we carry them over into other curricular areas.

Take an instructional walk later in the school day, at a time when teachers do not typically teach language arts. Do you see these instructional practices occurring in other subject areas? If you notice teachers with effective integration strategies in place, take the opportunity to compliment them through a note, email, or comment after your visit. By focusing on the positives of integration, teachers may become even more intentional about the integration of subject areas within their classroom. Use the specifics in the following sections as the basis of your comments.

Read-Alouds

When doing a read-aloud in social studies, teachers can be deliberate in thinking aloud and highlighting their own metacognition for students. In addition to the content, they can take the opportunity to talk about morphemes, vocabulary, or fluency. These intentional conversations do not detract from the lessons; they strengthen them. Not only will they help students understand and access the information we are teaching, they will also help solidify the strategies for students to transfer to independent use.

Reading aloud material in the content areas is also helpful because the vocabulary sometimes makes the text more difficult. Some students might not be able to decode or recognize the words on their own, but they could be able to understand the content.

Shared Reading

Shared reading is another effective way to read content area material with students. With text displayed on an interactive whiteboard or read from a textbook, teachers and students can read the text together, with the teacher providing as much support as necessary.

Guided Reading

If we know there are students who will struggle to read and comprehend, say, the science article we are teaching later in the day, then during guided reading we can bring these students together to read that article. By the time we get to science class, we will have already provided some support to them: previewing and discussing the format of the text, the vocabulary, and the content itself. Using this structure with content-area material can empower our students and build confidence in the process.

Partner Reading

Students can learn to support one another as readers in the content areas. Rather than expect them to read something on their own, perhaps we strategically pair students to read a small amount of text together and then discuss the content.

Other Scaffolds to Improve Comprehension

Scaffolds, such as frontloading with images, reciprocal teaching, conversation round tables, and connect–extend–challenge, can also support our students with content-area text. I chose these thinking routines or structures because they are especially effective with content-area curriculum, but be aware that there are many other such strategies that your teachers might use.

As a leader in your school, consider incorporating one of these strategies into a staff meeting or professional development opportunity. There tends to be a mix of novice and seasoned teachers in any staff grouping. For some teachers, these strategies might be new; for others, this could act as a refresher. Regardless, modelling effective strategies is always a good use of time because we know that teachers are more likely to try something with their students after they have tried it themselves!

Frontloading with Images

Frontloading with images is a powerful strategy and, incidentally, an opportunity to focus on viewing as one of the six strands of language.

Frontloading with images is a strategy explained in *Subjects Matter* by Daniels and Zemelman. Before reading content-area text or beginning a new unit of study, teachers provide students with images connected to the topic or concept. The images can be revealed either all at once or one at a time. As students look at the images, they are asked to think about what they see and articulate what they notice. Students often build on each other's thoughts. "Then, once we have built background knowledge and evoked curiosity, we can make a better transition to printed material" (Daniels and Zemelman 2014, 100). Although this is a simple strategy, it quickly generates conversation and activates prior knowledge about the topic. I wonder if we might have better understood the passage about cricket on page 101 if we had first seen images of the game, and if those images had labels.

Reciprocal Teaching

The strategy of reciprocal teaching was first introduced in the 1980s by Annemarie Sullivan Palincsar and Ann L. Brown in an effort to assist students with comprehension. It has been modified in many ways over the years, but the basic premise remains the same, with a focus on four strategies: predicting, clarifying, questioning, and summarizing. The teacher scaffolds the learning to help students become more efficient and aware of each of the strategies at work while reading. Typically, students work in groups of four and use these strategies to monitor their understanding before, during, and after reading. Once students are familiar with the four strategies, each student assumes a teaching role, guiding their peers through one of the four strategies as they stop periodically while reading. Groups of four are most natural in an elementary classroom, as teachers often assign each student one role on a given day. I have also seen it adapted for use within partner reading. Regardless of group size, the practice with peers enables students to rehearse each strategy.

Reciprocal teaching has been highly effective in classrooms of any age group and with a variety of student needs. As Fisher, Frey, and Hattie (2016) explain, "researchers have found it to be effective with students with disabilities, English learners, and bilingual students" (98). The eventual goal is that students will use these strategies organically when they are reading on their own; this structure provides the scaffolding needed to get there.

Conversation Round Tables

During a session with Fisher and Frey a few years ago, attendees were led through a conversation round table. I was drawn to this strategy immediately because it engages students in many elements of language learning with content-area text.

Title of text:	Name:
1. My notes	2. What _____ said
My independent summary	
3. What _____ said	4. What _____ said

Students work in groups of four, each with a sheet divided into four boxes, like the sample above. They begin by independently reading a passage (e.g., a few paragraphs, an article, a textbook page) and then write jot notes about the content of the passage in the top left box. Even this first step requires significant practice on the part of students; note-taking and summarizing do not always come easily. After students complete their own notes, one by one, each shares their ideas with the group. As they do, the other students jot down each person's ideas in the corresponding boxes. After everyone has shared, students write a short summary of the text, including any new understandings of the content they have gleaned from listening to their peers.

This process honors the ideas of each person, demonstrates that we have variations in understanding, and shows students that our understandings can change.

Connect–Extend–Challenge

This framework is somewhat similar to the KWL chart (what I *Know*, what I *Want* to know, what I *Learned*) that many teachers use with students. However, I appreciate the language used in this version, as it helps students think about their learning.

Connect Information I already know	**Extend** New information learned	**Challenge** Questions I have

This thinking routine was developed as part of the *Visible Thinking Project* at Project Zero, Harvard Graduate School of Education.

After reading text or watching a video, students jot down their thinking. In the first column—Connect—students describe how the ideas they read or heard about connect with what they already know; in effect, they are articulating their background knowledge on the topic. In the second column—Extend—students write down the new information they have learned; they consider how the information has *extended* their thinking. In the third column—Challenge—students reflect on challenges, questions, or confusions that might have arisen from the new information.

Enhancing Vocabulary Development Across the Curriculum

We have come to understand the importance of vocabulary to assist students with reading comprehension. As we discussed on page 60, there are Three Tiers of Vocabulary. A focus on Tier Two Words (academic words that cross disciplinary boundaries) and Tier Three Words (content-specific words) are both essential. As Fisher, Frey, and Hattie (2016) remind us, "Learning a word requires not just exposure, but also repetition, contextualization, and authentic reasons to use the terminology in discussion, reading, and writing" (50). The one-time teaching of a word is not enough. Repeated exposures in various contexts are essential if we want students to carry the words into their long-term memories.

Does vocabulary instruction have to occur exclusively within language arts? Most certainly not. I encourage teachers to bring such activities and strategies as word sorts, concept circles, and generative sentences into any subject area. Social studies and science might be great places to start! Once again, consider modelling one of these strategies during a meeting. Or if you have noticed a teacher using one of these strategies with students, invite that teacher to model the strategy at a meeting or record a lesson with their students.

After you introduce one of these strategies during a meeting, give teachers time to create their own version to use with students. If they are left to plan it at another time, they might get busy and forget. Give them time during the meeting!

Word Sorts

Word sorts are an effective way to get students thinking more deeply about the vocabulary and the overall concepts we are teaching.

For example, if my Grade 4 class is studying plant growth in science, perhaps I give my students this list of words: *air, seedling, stem, sunlight, seed, water, leaves, nutrients, sprout, flowers, roots, plant*. In this list, there are many words that most students would be familiar with already; there are also a few words that might be fairly new to them, such as *seedling, nutrients*, and *sprout*. Students are asked to sort these words into three columns.

Once they have sorted the words, they are asked to articulate why they sorted them the way they did. Depending on the grade and the circumstance, I might also have them develop headings for each column. When I created this particular list of words, I had three categories in mind: *parts of a plant, plant requirements for growth*, and *the life cycle of a plant*. Some students recognized these concepts from my recent teaching and organized the words in the same way.

In the sample below, the student sorted the words the way I had intended, with slight variations in the headings. She also numbered the stages within the life cycle without being asked. An eraser was a necessary part of this process for the student, as she revised her thinking along the way.

What a plant needs to grow	Parts of a plant	Stages of a plant
air	stem	seedling ③
sunlight	leaves	seed ①
water	flowers	sprout ②
nutrients	roots	plant ④

I typically gravitate to open-ended word sorts, as they reveal the different ways our students think. However, if we want students to sort the words according to their meaning and not word structure, we can certainly specify this for them.

Perhaps other students grouped the words in different ways. I do not expect all students to sort the words into the categories that I created, as long as they can articulate their *why*. Another student may categorize this list of words according to syllables: *air, stem, seed, leaves, sprout, roots*, and *plant* are all one syllable words, after all. *Seedling, sunlight, water*, and *flowers* are all two syllables. *Nutrients* is the only word that is three syllables. Would this sort by a student be incorrect? Not at all! This student's sort reflects another element of words that we have previously discussed in class.

When I invite teachers to try this strategy with me, they are often surprised at the level of thinking involved. The sorts are not difficult to create, but they create meaningful opportunities for students to think and talk about a concept.

In the process of sorting, all students are engaged in thinking about the meaning of each word, the relationships between the words, and the concepts we have been focusing on as a class. As you can see, a word sort is much more than an activity of recall. Some teachers might wonder *Is this an effective use of time in science class?* Most definitely. It will deepen students' understanding of both vocabulary and content. As part of their thinking process, they also happen to use many strands of language arts: reading the words, using oral language to articulate their thinking, and listening to other points of view.

Concept Circles

Rather than having students simply memorize the meaning of vocabulary words, concept circles provoke them to think about the meaning of the words and the relationships between them. Concept circles can be used in a variety of ways. With elementary-aged students, I divide the circle into four parts with a smaller circle in the centre. I fill in three parts of the circle with words or phrases we have been using in social studies, for example: *protest, elections, freedom*. The fourth section of the circle and the centre of the circle are left blank. Students are asked to think about the connection between the three words and determine the concept (in this case, *democracy*) which they would write in the centre. Then, they are also challenged to think of a fourth word or phrase that connects to the other words in the circle (e.g., *equality, representation, rule by the people, freedom of the press*). Once again, to strengthen the routine and deepen the learning, students would be expected to articulate their thinking to a peer.

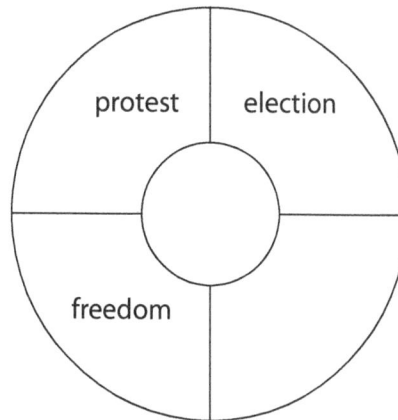

Although this example demonstrates how concept circles can be used with older students, concept circles are just as effective with younger students. If a Grade 2 class is learning about liquids in science, for example, the three given words could be *water, orange juice*, and *milk*. The circle in the middle is left blank for the concept (*liquids*) as well as the fourth space where students could insert another liquid of their choosing.

Concept circles can be used during many points in our instruction: at the beginning of a class for a review of the day before, as a check for understanding part-way through a unit of study, or even at the end of a unit.

Generative Sentences

Another strategy introduced to me by Fisher and Frey is the idea of generative sentences. In some classrooms, students are asked to write sentences with their spelling words. Although the intention is good—to practice using the words in a sentence—this task is not always an effective use of our students' time. In one class where I observed this task, a Grade 4 student wrote the same sentence for each word, just replacing the word itself. Did he know the meaning of the words? Not likely. Did he gain anything from the exercise? Not really. Was he engaged in his learning? He didn't appear to be; in fact, his intent seemed to be to finish as quickly as possible. After seeing this, I introduced the idea of generative sentences to his teacher. A few weeks later, she shared that it changed both her practice and student engagement entirely.

What are generative sentences? Students still write sentences with words the teacher provides; however, students are given specific parameters. This chart shows an example of the specifics I might give to my students.

Word	Position	Length of Sentence
habitat	3rd	> five words
mammal	6th	= six words
adapt	4th	< ten words
survival	1st	< seven words

Students at all grade levels, including our Grade 1 students in the later part of the year, can engage in this activity. However, teachers may have to simplify and scaffold for the younger students when they first introduce the task.

Generative sentences bring together our literacy learning and our learning of content area vocabulary. Because students are told the position of the word in the sentence and the length of the sentence, they are forced to experiment to see what makes sense. Suddenly grammar comes into play. Students must keep the word in its current form (they cannot make a noun plural or put a verb in past tense, for example) so you will often hear students playing around with the sentence out loud before they find something that makes sense. Through this activity, we give our students another opportunity to practice using their new vocabulary, but they are doing so more authentically.

In every class where I have introduced generative sentences, students tend to see them both as a challenge and as fun. A list of four words is often enough, as the sentences take some time to complete. Another benefit of generative sentences: students often use other words from the unit of study within their sentences.

Morphology

In Chapter 5 we discussed morphology: the study of words, how they are formed, and how they relate to other words. Once teachers are aware of morphemes, they begin to notice them everywhere. And in fact, the content areas of our curriculum are full of them. For example, consider these numeric prefixes: *uni-, bi-, duo-, tri-, quad-, quint-, sept-, oct-, non-, dec-, cent-, mill-*! Other common morpheme roots in math are *fract, equ,* and *circ*.

Are you curious about frequently used morphemes?

Prefixes: *pre-, re-, un-, dis-, in-, im-*
Suffixes: *-ed, -ing, -ly, -less, -er, -est, -ful, -ment*
Roots: *bio, astro, geo, form, port, struct, vis, aqua*

At some point during a staff meeting, you are likely going to discuss phonics with your staff. Take this opportunity to talk morphemes too! Ask them what morphemes they recognize in the words *phoneme* and *grapheme*. As I mentioned in Chapter 5, the Greek root *phon* means "sound," whereas *graph* means "writing." How do these roots connect to the words' meanings? What other words can your teachers think of that use these morphemes? Give them a few examples, such as *microphone* and *symphony*, and *paragraph* and *biography*, but then challenge them to create as long a list as they can.

When I have engaged teachers in an activity such as this, they tend to get excited and sometimes even competitive! The activity becomes one they remember and therefore one they are more likely to introduce to their students. After the activity, ask teachers to think about the vocabulary in their content-area curriculum. What morphemes do they notice?

What about a science lesson on thermal energy? A teacher familiar with morphemes could talk about the word *thermal* and highlight the root *therm* for students. Students could generate a list of words that use this root. Perhaps the class generates this list of words: *thermometer, thermos, thermostat, hypothermia.* Then students turn-and-talk with a partner to make predictions about the meaning of the root. With the list of words in front of them, many students will be able to come up with the answer. Moving forward, then, they know that when they encounter a word with the morpheme *therm,* it has something to do with heat.

An awareness of morphology enables students to develop visual acuteness and recognize word parts to help them determine the meaning of the words in all areas of the curriculum. Empowering your teachers in this area will enable them to empower your students.

Writing to Learn Across the Curriculum

When I first introduced freewriting to my students, my intention was to break through their reluctance and simply get them writing. However, there were many other unexpected positive outcomes. One such outcome was realizing the power of the process in helping students construct meaning in all areas of the curriculum; i.e., writing to learn. One particular moment stands out for me: after we had finished freewriting and were reading over our writing, one of my students exclaimed, "I didn't know I thought that!" It was such as fascinating moment and reminded me that writing is often thinking on the page. Others agree. In Isaac Asimov's words: "Writing, to me, is simply thinking through my fingers." And Barack Obama once said,

> Writing has been an important exercise to clarify what I believe, what I see, what I care about, what my deepest values are. The process of converting a jumble of thoughts into coherent sentences makes you ask tougher questions.

Freewriting in the content areas provides students with the opportunity to think through the concepts, to process what they have learned, and to figure out how it connects to what they already know. This low-stakes writing—writing that will not be assessed and only shared if students choose—is a powerful process.

In the elementary edition of *Tools for Teaching Conceptual Understanding*, Julie Stern (2018) reminds us,

> We want our students to not only retain what we've taught them, but relate it to other things they encounter, using each new situation to add nuance and sophistication to their thinking. (9)

Freewriting helps us do this. For example, we might give students these two prompts: *I used to think…* and *But now I know….* In this case, I expect students to begin with the first prompt and then continue with the second. This is effective after watching a video, at the end of a unit, or after shared reading and discussion.

As discussed in Chapter 7, freewriting works best when our elementary students use a prompt. The prompts used when we are writing to learn are simple and straightforward. For example, after watching a science demonstration, we could put three prompts on the board: *I noticed…, I think…,* and *I wonder….* Students can move in and out of the prompts as they connect with them. Chapters 7 through 11 of *Freewriting with Purpose* address the idea of writing to learn across the curriculum and include many potential prompts and ways to use freewriting in each area of study.

If your teachers are familiar with the process of freewriting, challenge them to engage students in freewriting as a means of writing to learn. Then at a meeting discuss what they noticed about the process.

Digital Literacy

"The ability to create, navigate, and evaluate information on various digital platforms is generically called *digital literacy*." (Willingham 2017, 164)

Technology is a fascinating and fundamental part of our daily lives. The continual advances in technology astound me. Smart glasses help the blind to see and to receive real-time visual information about the world they interact with; bionic limbs respond to messages from the brain; Messenger RNA is used to create vaccines. The list is never-ending and additions can be made daily.

There is no doubt that technology has changed the way our students interact with their world and even the ways they read and write, and not all the changes are positive. Constant interactions with the digital world change our ability to focus, our need for stimulation, even our urge to multitask. It is therefore essential that we provide time for our students to slow down their thinking and interact with the printed page. These are skills we do not want them to lose.

In *Reader, Come Home: The Reading Brain in a Digital World*, Maryanne Wolf (2018) suggests,

> The most important contribution of the invention of written language to the species is a democratic foundation for critical, inferential reasoning and reflective capacities. This is the basis of a collective conscience. If we in the twenty-first century are to preserve a vital collective conscience, we must ensure that all members of our society are able to read and think both deeply and well. We will fail as a society if we do not educate our children and reeducate all of our citizenry to the responsibility of each citizen to process information vigilantly, critically, and wisely across media. (200–201)

Parents of elementary-aged children often question the use of technology in the classroom. For some, there is too much of a focus on technology. For others, not enough. Think about the uses of technology as discussed in this chapter when formulating how you might respond to parent questions.

As important as it is that we maintain our interactions with the printed page, it is also essential that we teach our students (and adults) how to navigate the digital world. Balance is key.

Interacting with Digital Text

Students now engage with a wider assortment of text than ever before. In fact, the definition of *text* is ever expanding. Each time our language-arts curriculum is updated, additional forms of text are added. As teachers, we must embed digital text and these expanded forms of text into our classrooms. We must teach students how to read and interpret a variety of digital text. We would be remiss not to.

Digital Citizenship

To ensure the safety of our elementary-age students, digital citizenship is an important topic to discuss. Consider bringing in a guest speaker on the topic: a police officer or other expert in the field. In my experience, these presentations are best held in individual classrooms (rather than with the whole school) to create a safe environment in which to ask questions and engage in meaningful discussion.

Marie Holmes (2022) writes about a study published in *Frontiers in Psychology* in August 2022. Researchers at Comenius University in Slovakia wanted to test adolescents to see if they could recognize both genuine and fake messages in online media. The sample consisted of 300 secondary-school students. Researchers provided students with a variety of health-related messages, some true, others not. They found that 41% of the participants were not able to distinguish between fake and true messages. This study confirms my own experience with students as they strive to become discerning readers of digital text.

Taking the time to talk about the sources and the validity of messages is critical both for regular consumption and also for our students' research. Fisher, Frey, and Hattie (2016) concur:

> The Internet is an excellent source for digital material, but it is fraught with problems that can derail student projects. Chief among them are issues of credibility and accuracy of information. (96)

In elementary schools, teachers must carefully consider how their students will research information. When our goal is research, we can find credible sources and sites ahead of time for students to reference. When our goal is to critically evaluate websites and information, this is best learned at the elementary level by working through the process together, reading and analyzing shared text. Ultimately, we want students to be critical consumers and users of information independently, but it is a skill that takes both guidance and time to develop.

Our teachers should also be critical consumers when they seek out resources to support their teaching. New teachers, or teachers new to a grade, sometimes gravitate to resources that seem a quick fix but might not be grounded in research or considered best practice. Conversations about resources at a staff meeting can help ensure teachers feel supported and prepared for their planning and instruction.

Writing on a Device

As much as I love writing on my computer, I know this is not always best practice for students, especially our elementary-aged students. Initially they should learn to compose their written work on paper. Eventually they will learn the value of word processing and all it enables us to do. But for young students still learning to write, the addition of a computer changes the process entirely.

With good intentions, administrators sometimes purchase one-to-one devices for primary students. And yet these students are still learning the basics of reading and writing. Shared access to devices typically gives primary students enough time with technology at those early grade levels.

Pay particular attention to the use of technology in your classrooms. How is digital technology being used?

Teachers should be intentional about how devices are used with our youngest students. When writing new content, our students' inability to type proficiently is a hindrance to the generation of ideas. For elementary students, journal writing, freewriting, and reader response are all ideal opportunities to print or handwrite. Within these forms of writing, we want our students to explore emotional connections, leave their mark on the page, and form beginning ideas, all without the worry of an end product. The relationship between a writer and the pen or pencil as writing tool lends itself to this type of thinking on the page.

As our students get older, it is for longer forms of writing or writing we spend considerable time revising and editing that the tool of the computer is especially useful. For the process of revision, we can teach our students how to use word processing to insert, move, or delete text with ease.

For the process of editing, we can teach our students the features embedded within word processing programs that assist us with spelling, grammar, and punctuation. But all this can happen in good time. Our elementary students should learn these processes on paper first before they transition to writing on the computer.

Digital technologies like text messaging have influenced writing in other ways, too. Does shorthand or textese—BRB instead of *be right back*—change the way our students write in the classroom? Does the lack of punctuation in their text messages trickle into other writing as well? Only if we let it. As teachers, we should discuss the purpose, audience, and intent of our writing. Because text messages serve a different purpose—quick, casual communication—we can acknowledge that a lack of traditional conventions may be acceptable. Students should be clear, however, that our expectations for proper conventions in other writing remains.

Digital literacy has become an important literacy to add to our classroom instruction. Our teaching of digital literacy will continue to evolve along with the technology.

Instructional Walk Considerations: Literacy in Content Areas

After reading and thinking more about literacy in the content areas, consider these questions on your next instructional walk:

- Do you see integration at work within your school, or do teachers feel the pressure to teach in silos?
- How are teachers using literacy within the content areas to ensure students are reading and writing for authentic purposes?
- Do teachers see the importance of building their students' background knowledge? How can you tell?
- How are teachers bringing digital literacy into their classrooms?
- Is there a balance between writing with pencil on paper and writing with technology within your classrooms?
- Are upper elementary students learning specific word-processing features that can assist them with their writing?

Talk Time: Literacy in Content Areas

Take some time to read and think about this passage and these questions before discussing them with your colleagues. Choose a specific topic about literacy in the content areas that is most timely for you, or discuss the set(s) of questions decided upon by your school team.

In language arts, we learn to read and write. In the content areas, we read and write to help us learn and understand new material. Why not bring these two together, capitalizing on authentic opportunities to use the literacy skills we are learning throughout the day?

Integration

- How do you use such instructional practices as read-alouds, shared reading, guided reading, and partner reading to support students with content-area text? Could you include them more often?
- In what other ways do you intentionally bring literacy into other areas of the curriculum?
- How might you be even more deliberate about capitalizing on the power of integration? Consider these areas specifically: reading, vocabulary development, morphology, and writing.

Improving Comprehension of Content Area Text

- How can you support your students with reading content-area materials? What specific strategies do you currently use? What else could you try?
- Why is it important to help students build background knowledge? How can we do this?

Digital Literacy

- What do you notice about your students when they engage in digital text?
- How do you support your students as they interact with a variety of text types, including digital text?
- Do your students have the opportunity to print/handwrite each day? For which types of tasks or writing?
- If you teach upper elementary students, are they beginning to use computers to write some of the time? For which types of written tasks? Do you teach your students how to use the tools available to them on the computer?

9

Supporting Literacy Success for All

"Literacy is among the major antidotes for poverty."
— Doug Fisher, Nancy Frey, and John Hattie

An Antidote to Poverty

Literacy changes lives. Without it, children and adults are more vulnerable to poverty. They are more likely to be unemployed or underemployed. They are more likely to be paid less, and more vulnerable to ill health and malnutrition. In Canada, thankfully, children have access to school and education. It's law, in fact. Unfortunately, this does not necessarily mean that all students leave our classrooms skilled in literacy. As Seidenberg (2017) reminds us,

> Reading is one of the few activities you do every day whether you want to or not. Street signs, menus, e-mails, Facebook posts, novels, ingredients in Chex Mix. You read for work, for school, for pleasure; because you have to, because you want to, because you can't help it. (3)

It is essential that we do what we can to support our readers—all readers—so they can function and interact fully in society. Your role is vital in the success of the students in your school.

According to *ABC Life Literacy Canada*,

> 48% of adult Canadians have literacy skills that fall below a high school level, which negatively affects their ability to function at work and in their personal lives. 17% of Canadians score at or below the lowest level, where they may, for example, be unable to read the dosage instructions on a medicine bottle (OECD Programme for the International Assessment of Adult Competencies, 2013).

Many factors contribute to these numbers. And low literacy skills in the home often lead the next generation to further challenges with literacy. As Willingham (2017) says,

"Without well-developed reading skills, children cannot participate fully in classroom learning. They are at much greater risk for school failure and lifelong problems with employment, social adjustment, and personal autonomy. Literate cultures expect literacy of everyone." (Moats 2020, 7)

Students from disadvantaged backgrounds show a characteristic pattern of reading achievement in school; they make good progress until around fourth grade, and then suddenly fall behind. The importance of background knowledge to comprehension gives us insight into this phenomenon. (128)

If parents themselves have low literacy skills, if oral language and reading are not a priority in the home, if issues of poverty create different priorities, the cycle continues. As educators, we play an important role in breaking this cycle. The question is *How do we pull children out of this cycle?* How do we ensure that all students leave elementary school with the foundations needed for literacy success throughout their lives?

Avoiding the Blame Game

It is certainly frustrating when our efforts to teach students to read and write do not result in success for all. I have worked with students, both in the classroom and during intervention, who didn't make the progress I hoped to see. But we cannot blame our readers. And we certainly cannot blame their families. We have acknowledged the complexity of reading and the many factors that contribute to reading comprehension. The title of Robin Bright's book, *Sometimes Reading is Hard*, reminds us of the challenges of learning to read. Bright (2021) also makes an important distinction:

> Notice the difference between these two statements: "Sometimes reading is hard" and "Maria is a struggling reader." When we say the first statement, we help teachers and students understand that challenges are a normal part of reading and that these challenges do not mean there is something wrong with the reader. When we acknowledge that sometimes reading is hard, the implication is that teachers and students can work together to figure out what to do next. (14)

I appreciate this approach. Let's not dwell on the problems, let's figure out a solution.

Our own perspectives and perceptions about our students who have difficulty with reading are more important than we might realize. Fisher, Frey, and Hattie (2016) point to Hattie's research: "Teachers' expectations of students become the reality for students" (16). I know teachers who believe that every child can reach their potential, and their actions support this. They do everything they can to help their students succeed, including continual learning and adjusting their own practice. Hattie's research confirms that the opposite is true as well: "Yes, teachers with low expectations are particularly successful at getting what they expect" (16). If we have students with poor attendance or a lack of home support, we can't blame their circumstances and presume that these students won't learn. The same premise applies: let's not dwell on the problems; let's figure out a solution.

When we know better, we can do better!

As administrators, it is also essential that we not blame our teachers. Most of our teachers are doing the best they can in the situations they are in, with the knowledge they have. But that's the point, we must ensure that our elementary teachers have ongoing opportunities for professional learning based on the research. They cannot adjust their practice if they do not understand the need for change or are not given opportunities to learn how. And we cannot assume that our teachers are all engaged in best practice or have a full understanding of the research. One of my goals with this book has been to provide you with the insight to recognize best practice for literacy instruction and support teachers in its absence.

Prevention First

As much as possible, our goal is to meet our students' needs through universal programming: planning and instruction, best practice that will support as many students as possible within the classroom environment. Moats (2020) suggests:

> According to the convergent findings of numerous studies, classroom instruction that builds phoneme awareness, phonic decoding skills, text reading fluency, vocabulary, and various aspects of comprehension is the best antidote for reading difficulty. (19–20)

Kilpatrick (2016) also brings a positive voice to the table in regards to prevention:

> The exciting news is that we can prevent most reading difficulties. Strangely, that is old news among researchers. This prevention phenomenon has been demonstrated in numerous studies over the years, reports of which almost never cross the divide between reading researchers to our K–12 classrooms. (116)

There's the challenge: bringing the instructional strategies guided by research into classroom practice. Teachers cannot continue to do what they've always done just because they've always done it. Recognizing the research and changing practice accordingly is essential.

The VAKT Strategy

As part of prevention, teachers should also consider the VAKT strategy. This strategy recommends presenting information using multiple senses: visual, auditory, and kinesthetic or tactile. In her book *Finding a Place for Every Student*, Cheryll Duquette (2022) says,

> … most students learn best when the material is presented visually (words, pictures, videos, diagrams, demonstrations), accompanied by oral instruction (auditory), and followed by kinesthetic/tactile (touching, manipulating, printing/writing/typing, doing the task). (26)

To accommodate these different modalities, literacy teachers in elementary school will often request manipulatives for student use: magnetic letters, individual whiteboards, and letter tiles, for instance. The same is true in math. If such tools help prevent learning challenges, they are certainly worth the cost. Paying staff to provide intervention year after year is much costlier.

When Intervention Is Necessary

There will be times when teachers come to you in frustration, when they notice students not progressing as expected, despite their best efforts. If you know those

As an administrator, consider what you will do to ensure that all teachers, regardless of their years of experience or their expertise, will have access to the latest research and to classroom practices guided by this research. These decisions will have a direct impact on the amount of intervention required at your school.

teachers are doing everything they can in the classroom to support their students, then intervention might be necessary. The Response to Intervention (RTI) model has become popular for guiding intervention methods throughout North America. This model includes three tiers of intervention.

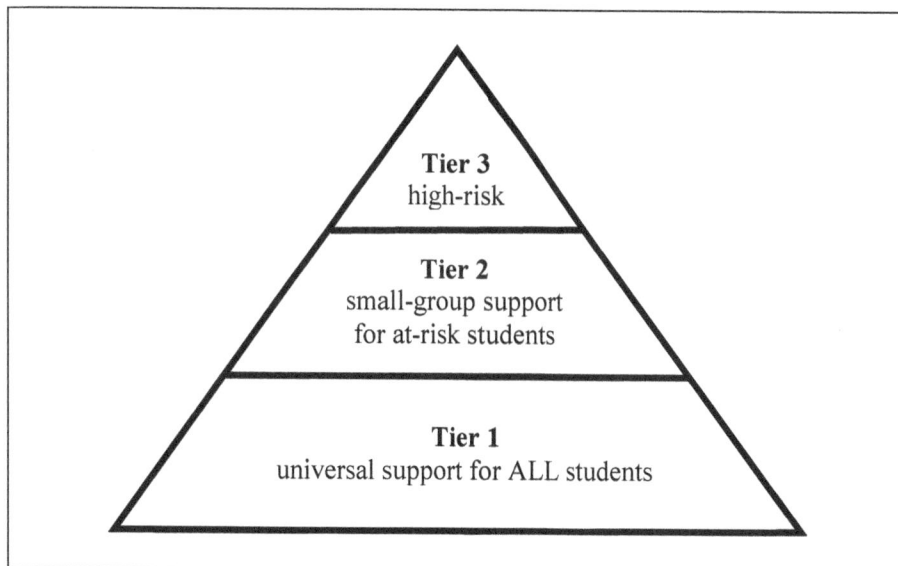

Tier 1 refers to the explicit, systematic instruction and differentiated support that occurs within our classrooms. For maximum effectiveness, the educational practices should be grounded in research.

Tier 2 refers to small-group intervention. Students who are not responding to Tier 1 instruction receive targeted small-group support three to five times each week, with the ultimate goal of becoming successful with Tier 1 support. Tier 2 intervention should also be evidence-based.

Students who do not respond to Tier 2 invention might require individualized, or Tier 3, support. These students would be considered high-risk; therefore, this tier is the most intense level of RTI.

In his book *Equipped for Reading Success*, Kilpatrick (2016) outlines the types of support provided at each level. He also says, "You will note much overlap between the levels. All involve the key components of orthographic mapping. By its very nature, RTI is just a process and a framework" (123). His book provides both the strategies and content that can be used within the framework; I highly recommend it to those looking for specific intervention strategies.

Scheduling Tier 2 and Tier 3 Intervention

Intervention is most effective with our youngest learners. Whenever possible, we want to provide intervention in Kindergarten and Grades 1 and 2. The earlier the better. As students fall farther behind in word reading, their fluency will be compromised and their struggles will become more complex. The more complex their challenges, the more difficult they are to overcome, and the greater the frustration for our students. If students in the older grades do require intervention, we provide it. However, if we think in the long term, we see that high-quality classroom practice based on research should prevent many of the concerns that now arise for our older students.

"Teachers who are most effective with struggling readers have both content knowledge and practical skill and are more inclined to use direct, systematic, explicit, structured language methods for those who do not learn easily." (Moats 2020, xxii)

If students are taken for intervention with a teacher other than their own, it is important that the two teachers talk regularly about the strategies being used. The classroom teacher can then reinforce what is being taught during intervention.

When students require Tier 2 or 3 intervention, we must think carefully about when to provide that intervention. In *Reading in the Wild*, Donalyn Miller (2014) gives us this to consider:

> When providing reading time at school, we must ensure that all students receive equal access. Administrators, literacy coaches, specialists, and teachers must consider the importance of this reading culture when determining how and when to serve special education and at-risk students. Too often reading intervention specialists pull students who require additional reading support out of class during independent reading time. Disregarding the effect of independent reading time on students' reading achievement undermines our intervention efforts over the long haul. (10)

The students who struggle with reading are often the ones who do not identify themselves as readers. They may also be the ones who do not come from literacy-rich homes. These students deserve the same opportunities to have positive associations with books and reading as other students. We could argue that they need these positive associations most of all! Give these students the time to read independently with their class and take them out for intervention at another time. And these students should also have access to the Tier 1 supports provided during language-arts instruction, so avoid this time for intervention whenever possible.

Taking students out of subjects they deem fun—physical education, music, and art, for example—could also have negative consequences. Likely, these struggling readers are working hard to cope with everything going on in the academic classroom. We should not deny our at-risk students the opportunities to excel and enjoy learning, which for some might occur only in the areas of the curriculum where reading and writing are not the focus.

Identifying the Gaps

When thinking about the content of intervention, I return to Kilpatrick (2016):

> Rather than labeling students *reading disabled*, *learning disabled*, or *dyslexic*, it makes more sense to look at what determines skilled reading and find out which skill area or areas are holding these students back…. Would it not make more sense to evaluate these key skill areas and address any weaknesses directly, rather than considering him or her "disabled?" A term like "disabled" implies that the student is destined to struggle in reading. (120)

Rather than assume that a student will not be able to learn to read, we determine *how* they can. Kilpatrick outlines seven skills that can help us understand our students' strengths and weaknesses: oral vocabulary, letter–sound knowledge, phoneme awareness, oral blending, rapid automatized naming, working memory, and phonic decoding. By creating a student profile around these skills, we can address the specific needs of our struggling readers. The various screening tools discussed on page 74 in Chapter 6 can help determine specific student needs.

As an administrator, you realize that intervention is expensive. So when it is necessary, you want to ensure the most efficient use of time. By working with your staff to develop ways to recognize student gaps, instruction can be better targeted for student success.

English Language Learners

Because of their circumstances, most students learning English will need support to some extent. Although their language comprehension in their first language might be quite strong, time, exposure, and direct instruction in English are needed. In addition to phonological awareness and phonemic awareness, our English Language Learners students need support with language comprehension to increase exposure to English vocabulary, word knowledge, and the structure and syntax of the language. Teachers should be acutely aware of building background knowledge and cultural competency for these students. Once again, the sooner we can provide intervention for our English Language Learners, the better.

Instructional Walk Considerations: Literacy Success for All

After reading and thinking more about how to support literacy success for all students, consider these questions on your next instructional walk:

- Do your teachers have knowledge of the research and strategies for best practice to prevent as many reading difficulties as they can? If not, what kind of support can be provided?
- Is the Response to Intervention (RTI) model something used within your district? How is it determined who will receive Tier 2 (small-group) and Tier 3 (individualized) intervention? How is the content of the intervention decided upon?
- If literacy intervention is provided within your school, does the teacher providing the intervention have the knowledge they need to support students?
- How can you facilitate the communication between the classroom teacher and the intervention teacher to ensure that skills and strategies are being transferred into the classroom environment?
- Consider the number of English Language Learners within your school. How are they being supported with phonological awareness, phonemic awareness, and overall language development?
- Are interpreters being accessed to communicate most effectively with parents of English Language Learners?

Talk Time: Literacy Success for All

Take some time to read and think about these questions before discussing them with your colleagues.

- Think about the students in your classroom who have the most difficulty with reading. What are you doing in the classroom to support and differentiate for these students? What is working? What do you find challenging about supporting these students?
- Do you feel knowledgeable about the research into the ways that students best learn to read? Why or why not?
- How might you determine the specific cause(s) of your students' difficulties with reading? What screeners or assessments could help with this?
- If you have students receiving Tier 2 support—small-group intervention with another teacher—how do you check their progress and reinforce the skills and strategies during your classroom instruction?

Pembroke Publishers ©2023 *Literacy Leadership Matters* by Karen Filewych ISBN 978-1-55138-361-3

10

Encouraging Home Literacy Experiences

"Children are made readers on the laps of their parents."
— Emilie Buchwald

What do you want students and parents to feel when they walk into your school? Your environment should not only be welcoming, but also demonstrate the value placed on learning and literacy. What is the first thing parents see when they enter? What about when they walk the halls? Are your priorities visible?

The decisions you make about your school demonstrate your priorities, too. If your decisions support literacy learning for all, parents will understand why money is allocated for English Language Learners and at-risk students. If they know that literacy is your priority, the parent council might support you by bringing in an author for an author visit or providing funding for classroom books or manipulatives. Education is a partnership. The more aligned we are as *home* and *school*, the better for our students.

Educating Parents

In elementary school, in particular, educators have considerable contact with parents. I view this as an opportunity. As much as we develop our students' skills and foster a love of reading and books at school, we want this to carry over into the home environment. For some students, it will happen quite naturally. For others, for a variety of reasons, it is not so easy. Sometimes parents don't understand the immeasurable value of reading in the home. Some parents are working multiple jobs and their focus is on day-to-day survival. Some might be dealing with family illness or addiction. We can't fully know the circumstances of our students or their parents.

With our students' best interests in mind—regardless of their home scenario—we can strive to educate parents: through newsletters or social media posts, during meet-the-teacher events or family literacy evenings. Some of the information you share with parents might be about events in your school or the instructional practices your teachers are using. When it comes to literacy, sharing quotes or statistics is often a good place to start. Following up with strategies is even better! You just might influence some families to be more deliberate with their time.

I invite you to share the statistics, quotes, or suggestions from this chapter with parents. (Please be sure to quote the source when you do.)

Home Reading Programs

Many elementary teachers set up home reading programs for their students. Sometimes these programs are quite formalized, especially with our youngest readers. Students sign out a book from the classroom each day, read it at home (to parents or siblings, if the students are young), return the book to school the next day, and then repeat the process. Home reading is meant as practice to reinforce what is being taught at school, and also as a little push to read at home. Sometimes home reading, especially in the upper elementary grades, is simply a request made of students without a formalized program: they are asked to read 20 to 30 minutes a night, for example.

There might be times when students bring the same book home for more than one day, sometimes purposefully and sometimes because—during the hectic nature of the day—they didn't have the opportunity to change their books. Parents have been known to complain that the same books are being sent home multiple times. As teachers, we know that repeated reading is an effective way to improve word recognition and fluency (and ultimately comprehension), but this must be clearly communicated to both students and parents. Students and parents might not realize the power of repeated readings.

Whatever the process looks like in your classrooms, teachers find most success when they communicate the procedure and expectations clearly to parents. Meet the Teacher Night (or its equivalent in your school) is often a wonderful opportunity to introduce both the logistics of the program and the rationale to parents. I have found the greatest buy-in when I share statistics with parents.

In their article "What Reading Does for the Mind," Cunningham and Stanovich (1998) write, "Although there are considerable differences in amount of reading volume in school, it is likely that differences in *out*-of-school reading volume are an even more potent source of the rich-get-richer and poor-get-poorer achievement patterns." According to the data taken from Table 3 of their article:

- A student in the thirtieth percentile reads independently for approximately 1.3 minutes per day.
- A student in the fiftieth percentile reads independently for approximately 4.6 minutes per day.
- A student in the eightieth percentile reads independently for approximately 14.2 minutes per day.
- A student in the ninety-eighth percentile reads independently for approximately 65.0 minutes per day.

Evidently, time spent reading matters. Although we can embed time into our classrooms, the more our students read beyond our classrooms, the better the results all around. When parents understand this, they are more likely to support and encourage reading in the home.

Sending Books Home

Many schools purchase books to be used specifically for home reading. Books are expensive, yes. And, yes, some books will be lost or damaged on the journey from school to home or back again. I would much rather lose a few books (and hope they are being read by someone) than not have books available for our students. The benefits of surrounding students with books and encouraging them to read at home is worth the expense.

If a student has become engaged in a book from the classroom library and wants to continue at home, I encourage them to take it back and forth. When students know that we value books, lost books are not a significant problem.

Reading Emergencies

I take a book along with me to appointments, knowing that I will probably have to wait. My perspective has changed from "When will they call me?" to "Wow, that was quick!" When I have a book with me, I enjoy the wait rather than resent it.

When I hear students talk about their evenings, I realize how scheduled many of them have become, with their activities and their siblings' activities. Students may say, "I don't have time to read," and believe this to be true. For a solution, I turn to Donalyn Miller once again. She describes what she calls "reading emergencies." She asks her students to think about all the time over the weekend, or the previous week, when they found themselves waiting. Her students have no problem generating a list: "Orthodontist's office, Little sister's soccer game, Sofa shopping with Mom, etc." (Miller 2014, 14). This leads to a discussion of how the time could have been different if they had a book with them. Then she challenges them to try it: "Take a book everywhere you go."

When students start carrying a book and using down-time to read—time previously spent waiting—they are pleasantly surprised at how easy it is to find time to read. It's important they realize that they don't have to read for 20 or 30 consecutive minutes. Five or seven or 10 minutes at a time works too: those minutes add up. Ultimately, it becomes less about the minutes and more about enjoying the time spent reading, engaged in a good book!

How might you share the idea of reading emergencies with the parents in your school? Do you want teachers to discuss the idea with their students? Or is this something you want to introduce to the parent community when they are gathered together? Perhaps both…

The Differences between Home Reading and Read-Alouds

"Children whose parents read to them frequently become familiar with the sophisticated vocabulary and syntax that appears in written rather than spoken language." (Wexler 2019, 34)

Parents often wonder about the differences between home reading and read-alouds. This, too, is something that can be explained to parents during a meet-the-teacher event. First and foremost, parents should understand that both are important daily practices, no matter the age of their children. Children are never too old to share in read-alouds with their parents, grandparents, or older siblings.

While home reading is the opportunity for children to practice their own reading, reading aloud *to* children generates many other positive outcomes. Read-alouds help children

"Reading aloud with children is known to be the single most important activity for building the knowledge and skills they will eventually require for learning to read."—Marilyn Adams

- develop phonological awareness, phonemic awareness, and an awareness of print
- increase their vocabulary
- improve their understanding of language: structure, grammar, syntax
- learn self-correction behaviors

- build background knowledge
- practice oral language skills through conversations about books
- discover the commonality of experience and develop a sense of empathy
- create bonds with the adults reading to them

If English is not the language spoken at home, encourage parents to read aloud to their children in their first language. This will support their children while promoting a love of literacy and a connection to their culture. As the children's English language proficiency increases, the children can also read aloud to their parents. Everyone wins!

Promoting Literacy Experiences in the Home

In addition to reading aloud, there are other experiences parents can be encouraged to engage in with their children. Social media posts are a wonderful way to provide parents with ideas to inspire literacy in the home. Or add a link on your school website where you can regularly share ideas. What do you share? Consider each of these sections for inspiration!

Library Visits

Book are expensive. Yet we have an incredible resource through our public libraries. Libraries are accessible to all, and are often the hub of a community. People who use the library when they are young are more likely to use it as adults.

I have a constant flow of books in and out of my home. I often go online and put books on hold; the books are brought to my closest library and I pick them up at my convenience. I intentionally share my library habits with my students. Why not share a "Did you know …" social media post about your local library? Check the website for upcoming events or for services they offer, such as homework help, reading programs, or access to a makerspace. Generate some library love in your community!

Invite your local public librarian to present to your students! Presentations are free and can be targeted to specific grade levels. Also consider presentations to your parent community. Do you have Meet-the-Teacher Night or a Book Fair coming up soon? Invite the librarian or a library representative to give a short presentation to parents, and then set up a table to assist families in signing up for library cards. This just might be the bridge needed to get some families to the library!

In *Reading Magic*, Mem Fox (2008) says, "Children who are read to early and regularly quickly acquire the skill of listening and the desire to hear stories. They understand the immense pleasures waiting for them in books and develop the ability to concentrate and relax." (33)

Talk, Talk, and More Talk!

As a classroom teacher, I often would send my students home with an assignment: *Tell your parents about… (the experiment we did today, the new words you learned, the book we read)*. It doesn't matter much what we request them to talk about; regardless of what they talk about, this is an excellent way for students to reinforce their learning and practice their oral language skills. I am transparent with students about why I request this of them. After all, we want them to think about the ways in which they learn.

I have had many parents share with me how this practice, which they first thought trivial, became a way for them to engage with their children in meaningful and purposeful ways. It shaped their conversations and extended much beyond my request.

Why not have teachers share this practice with parents on Meet-the-Teacher Night so parents know to expect it?

Family Game Nights

Encourage parents in your school to establish family game nights. There are many opportunities to read and engage in conversation while playing board games or card games. Why not highlight or encourage particular games? What are your family favorites? If you're not sure which would be age-appropriate, consider these as a starting point: *Guess Who?*, *Hedbanz*, *Kerplunk*, *Sequence for Kids*, and *Taboo Junior*.

Setting an Example

I recently saw a cartoon on Twitter. Picture this: two moms are sitting with their children on a park bench. One mom and her child are reading books. The other mom, with a phone in her hand, sits next to her son, who also has a phone in his hand. She turns to the first mom and says, "How do you get your child to read books?"

To me, this cartoon says it all. When children see the adults around them choosing reading as something to do, carrying books with them wherever they go, this becomes their norm.

Sharing Quotations

Throughout this chapter, I have included many quotations that would be appropriate to share with parents. A few more:

"A book is a gift you can open again and again." Garrison Keillor

"Reading is to the mind what exercise is to the body." Joseph Addison

"The more that you read, the more things you will know. The more that you learn, the more places you'll go." Dr. Seuss

"Reading makes all other learning possible. We have to get books in our children's hands early and often." Barrack Obama

"A reader lives a thousand lives before he dies." George R.R. Martin

"If you don't like to read, you haven't found the right book." J.K. Rowling

"Books are a uniquely portable magic." Stephen King

"Reading is an exercise in empathy; an exercise in walking in someone else's shoes for a while." Malorie Blackman

"There is no friend as loyal as a book." Ernest Hemingway

"Any book that helps a child to form a habit of reading, to make reading one of his deep and continuing needs, is good for him." Maya Angelou

"I read to be alone. I read so as not to be alone." Bich Minh Nguyen

Know Thy Impact

As the leader of a school, you have the opportunity to inspire and influence countless students, staff, and parents on a daily basis. In John Hattie's words: *know thy impact.*

The more you appreciate the complexity of teaching literacy and the more aware you are of the literacy practices and expectations within your school, the better equipped you are to be an effective literacy leader.

When parents share that they now read aloud to their children, you will know your words were heard. When teachers come to you for advice or suggestions, you will feel confident about the support you provide. When your school has literacy leaders supporting one another to be better, stronger, and more forward-thinking about the craft of teaching literacy, you will know that you have contributed to the creation of a community of learners. When students leave your school with a solid foundation in literacy, you will realize the role you played on their literacy journeys.

Glossary

Alphabetic Principle: the understanding that there are predictable relationships between written letters and spoken sounds. See page 50.

Articulatory Gestures: noticing what our mouth, lips, and tongue are doing as we produce a specific sound or *phoneme*. See page 52.

Blend: two letters that come together but each letter maintains their individual sounds; e.g., *fr, st, gl, sw.* See page 32.

Blending: combining *phonemes* to create a word; e.g., /d/ /i/ /g/ = dig. See page 52.

Concepts of Print: the understanding that text holds meaning, that letters form words, that print is read from top to bottom and left to right, how pages are turned, and so on. See page 64.

Digraph: two letters that come together and create a new sound; e.g., *sh, wh, th, ph.* See page 32.

Elkonin Boxes: an instructional tool used to help children improve their *phonemic awareness* by *segmenting* words into individual *phonemes.* See page 54.

Encoding: the ability to apply knowledge of letter–sound relationships to write words. See page 44.

Grapheme: the written representation of one sound (a letter or combination of letters). See page 30.

High-Frequency Words: the words most commonly used in the English language. They can be phonetically regular (e.g., *in, is, and, can, went*) or irregular (e.g., *the, of, have, was, should*). See page 56.

Morpheme: the smallest unit of meaning within a word. *Free morphemes* can stand alone; e.g., *girl, big, sleep. Bound morphemes* cannot stand alone or be used as an independent word. There are three types of bound morphemes that we typically teach our students: prefixes, suffixes, and roots. See page 55.

Morphology: the study of words, how they are formed, and how they relate to other words. See page 55.

Onset: the initial sound of any word; e.g., /d/ in *dog,* /tw/ in *twin.* See page 52.

Orthographic Mapping: the process used in the brain to map words (spelling, pronunciation, and meaning) into memory. See page 57.

Phoneme: the smallest unit of sound within a word. See page 52.

Phonemic Awareness: the awareness that words are made up of distinct sounds (phonemes). It is one subset of *phonological awareness.* See page 52.

Phonetic Decoding: the ability to apply knowledge of letter–sound relationships to correctly pronounce written words. See page 54.

Phonics: the knowledge that sounds (*phonemes*) are represented by letters or letter combinations (*graphemes*). See page 53.

Phonological Awareness: an awareness of the sound structure of words. It is an umbrella term that includes such subsets as *phonemic awareness,* syllables, *onset,* and *rime.* See page 52.

Plot Patterns: Structional patterns in the stories we read and write, e.g., transformation stories, circle stories, stuck stories, quest stories, competition stories. See page 96.

Prosody: the ability to read with expression, including elements such as phrasing, pitch, rhythm, intonation, tone, and emphasis. See page 66.

Rime: the string of letters that follow the *onset* sound; e.g., /og/ in *dog,* /in/ in *twin.* See page 52.

Scarborough's Reading Rope: In 2001, Dr. Hollis Scarborough published a graphic detailing the specific strands required to become a skilled reader; see visual on page 40.

Science of Reading: an extensive body of research on how our brains learn to read that includes scientific knowledge from experts in disciplines such as education, literacy, educational psychology, developmental psychology, and neurology. See page 51.

Segmenting: breaking a word apart into *phonemes*; e.g., *dad* = /d/ /a/ /d/. See page 30.

Sight Words: words that are instantly recalled from memory; they can be phonically regular or irregular. See page 56.

Sight-Word Vocabulary: each person's own set of vocabulary that they recognize from memory. See page 56.

Simple View of Reading: a theory proposed in 1986 by Philip Gough and William Tunmer: *Word Recognition × Language Comprehension = Reading Comprehension.* See page 39.

Professional Resources

Recommended Resources

For Teaching Reading

Beers, Kylene, and Robert E. Probst. 2017. *Disrupting Thinking: Why How We Read Matters*. New York, NY: Scholastic.

Bright, Robin. 2021. *Sometimes Reading is Hard: Using decoding, vocabulary, and comprehension strategies to inspire fluent, passionate, lifelong readers*. Markham, ON: Pembroke Publishers.

Burkins, Jan, and Kari Yates. 2021. *Shifting the Balance: 6 Ways to Bring the Science of Reading into the Balanced Literacy Classroom*. Portsmouth, NH: Stenhouse Publishers.

Miller, Donalyn. 2009. *The Book Whisperer: Awakening the Inner Reader in Every Child*. San Francisco, CA: Jossey-Bass.

Miller, Donalyn. 2014. *Reading in the Wild: The Book Whisperer's Keys to Cultivating Lifelong Reading Habits*. San Francisco, CA: Jossey-Bass.

For Teaching Writing

Culham, Ruth. 2003. *6+1 Traits of Writing: The Complete Guide Grades 3 and Up*. New York, NY: Scholastic.

Culham, Ruth. 2005. 6+1 Traits of Writing: The Complete Guide for the Primary Grades. New York, NY: Scholastic.

Filewych, Karen. 2017. *How Do I Get Them to Write? Explore the reading-writing connection using freewriting and mentor texts to motivate and empower students*. Markham, ON: Pembroke Publishers.

Filewych, Karen. 2019. *Freewriting with Purpose: Simple classroom techniques to help students make connection, think critically, and construct meaning*. Markham, ON: Pembroke Publishers.

For Teaching Phonics

Georgiou, George, and Kristy Dunn. 2023. *The Phonics Companion: 120 Lessons for Teachers*. Toronto, ON: Pearson Canada.

Willms, Heather and Giacinta Alberti. 2022. *This Is How We Teach Reading… And It's Working!: The What, Why, and How of Teaching Phonics in K-3 Classrooms*. Markham, ON: Pembroke Publishers.

For Teaching Word Study and Vocabulary

Allen, Janet. 2007. *Inside Words: Tools for teaching academic vocabulary, grades 4–12*. Portsmouth, NH: Stenhouse Publishers.

Beck, Isabel, Margaret McKeown, and Linda Kucan. 2013. *Bringing Words to Life: Robust Vocabulary Instruction*. New York, NY: The Guilford Press.

Swartz, Larry. 2019. *Word by Word: 101 ways to inspire and engage students by building vocabulary, improving spelling, and enriching reading, writing, and learning*. Markham, ON: Pembroke Publishers.

For General Instruction and Best Practice

Almarode, John, and Kara Vandas. 2019. *Clarity for Learning: Five Essential Practices that Empower Students and Teachers.* Thousand Oaks, CA: Corwin.

Fisher, Douglas, Nancy Frey, and John Hattie. 2017. *Teaching Literacy in the Visible Learning Classroom.* Thousand Oaks, CA: Corwin.

For Literacy Intervention

Kilpatrick, David. 2016. *Equipped for Reading Success: A Comprehensive, Step-by-Step Program for Developing Phonemic Awareness and Fluent Word Recognition.* Syracuse, NY: Casey & Kirsch Publishers.

Moats, Louisa, C. 2020. *Speech to Print: Language Essentials for Teachers.* Third Edition. Baltimore, MD: Paul H. Brookes Publishing Co.

References

ABC Life Literacy Canada. 2022. https://abclifeliteracy.ca/literacy-at-a-glance/

Adams, Marilyn J. 1994. *Beginning to Read: Thinking and Learning about Print.* Cambridge, MA: MIT Press.

Alberta Education. 2022. *English Language Arts and Literature.* Edmonton, AB: Alberta Education.

Almarode, John, and Kara Vandas. 2019. *Clarity for Learning: Five Essential Practices that Empower Students and Teachers.* Thousand Oaks, CA: Corwin.

Beck, Isabel, Margaret McKeown, and Linda Kucan. 2013. *Bringing Words to Life: Robust Vocabulary Instruction.* New York, NY: The Guilford Press.

Beers, Kylene, and Robert E. Probst. 2017. *Disrupting Thinking: Why How We Read Matters.* New York, NY: Scholastic.

Borba, Michele. 2016. *Unselfie: Why Empathetic Kids Succeed in Our All-About-Me World.* New York, NY: Touchstone.

Bright, Robin. 2021. *Sometimes Reading is Hard: Using decoding, vocabulary, and comprehension strategies to inspire fluent, passionate, lifelong readers.* Markham, ON: Pembroke Publishers.

Burkins, Jan, and Kari Yates. 2021. *Shifting the Balance: 6 Ways to Bring the Science of Reading into the Balanced Literacy Classroom.* Portsmouth, NH: Stenhouse Publishers.

Covey, Stephen. 2004. *The 7 Habits of Highly Effective People: Powerful Lessons in Personal Change.* New York, NY: Free Press.

Cunningham, Anne, and Keith Stanovich. 1998. "What Reading Does for the Mind." *American Educator,* Spring/Summer.

Daniels, Harvey and Steven Zemelman. 2014. *Subjects Matter: Exceeding Standards Through Powerful Content-Area Reading.* Portsmouth, NH: Heinemann.

Dehaene, Stanislas. 2010. *Reading in the Brain: The New Science of How We Read.* New York, NY: Penguin Group.

Duquette, Cheryll. 2022. *Finding a Place for Every Student: Inclusion practices, social belonging, and differentiated instruction in elementary classrooms.* Markham, ON: Pembroke Publishers.

Elbow, Peter. 1998. *Writing With Power: Techniques for Mastering the Writing Process.* New York, NY: Oxford University Press, Inc.

Fisher, Douglas, Nancy Frey, and John Hattie. 2016. *Visible Learning for Literacy: Implementing the Practices That Work Best to Accelerate Student Learning.* Thousand Oaks, CA: Corwin.

Fisher, Douglas, Nancy Frey, and John Hattie. 2017. *Teaching Literacy in the Visible Learning Classroom.* Thousand Oaks, CA: Corwin.

Fountas, Irene C, and Gay Su Pinnell. 2016. *The Fountas & Pinnell Literacy Continuum, Expanded Edition: A Tool for Assessment, Planning, and Teaching, Prek-8.* Portsmouth, NH: Heinemann.

Fox, Mem. 2008. *Reading Magic: Why Reading Aloud to Our Children Will Change Their Lives Forever.* New York, NY: Harper Paperbacks.

Fullan, Michael. 2007. Forward to Booth, David. *The Literacy Principal: Leading, supporting, and assessing reading and writing initiatives.* 2nd Edition. Markham, ON: Pembroke Publishers.

Goldberg, Natalie. 2005. *Writing Down the Bones: Freeing the Writer Within.* Boston, MA: Shambhala Publications, Inc.

Government of Nova Scotia. 2019. *English Language Arts P–6 at a glance.* Halifax: Department of Education and Early Childhood Development.

Hart, Melissa. 2019. *Better with Books: 500 Diverse Books to Ignite Empathy and Encourage Self-Acceptance in Tween and Teens.* Seattle, WA: Sasquatch Books.

Hattie, John. 2012. *Visible Learning for Teachers: Maximizing Impact on Learning*. New York, NY: Routledge.

Holmes, Marie. "Study Says Many Teens Can't Tell The Difference Between Read and Fake News." Huffpost, September 12, 2022. https://www.huffpost.com/entry/how-to-help-your-kids-spot-fake-news_l_631b4196e4b046aa02344b5d.

Johns, Jerry L., and Kristine H. Wilke. 2018. "High-Frequency Words: Some Ways to Teach and Help Students Practice and Learn Them." *Texas Journal of Literacy Education,* 6 (1).

Johnson, Brad and Hal Bowman. 2021. *Dear Teacher: 100 Days of Inspirational Quotes and Anecdotes.* New York, NY: Routledge.

Kilpatrick, David. 2016. *Equipped for Reading Success: A Comprehensive, Step-by-Step Program for Developing Phonemic Awareness and Fluent Word Recognition.* Syracuse, NY: Casey & Kirsch Publishers.

Miller, Donalyn. 2009. *The Book Whisperer: Awakening the Inner Reader in Every Child.* San Francisco, CA: Jossey-Bass.

Miller, Donalyn. 2014. *Reading in the Wild: The Book Whisperer's Keys to Cultivating Lifelong Reading Habits.* San Francisco, CA: Jossey-Bass.

Moats, Louisa, C. 2020. *Speech to Print: Language Essentials for Teachers.* Third Edition. Baltimore, MD: Paul H. Brookes Publishing Co.

Pearson, P. David, and Margaret C. Gallagher. 1983. "The Instruction of Reading Comprehension." *Contemporary Educational Psychology,* 8 (3): 317–44.

Riley, Benjamin. 2020. "Drawing on Reading Science without Starting a War." ACSD, 77 (5).

Roberts, Kate. 2018. *A Novel Approach: Whole-Class Novels, Student-Centered Teaching, and Choice.* Portsmouth, NH: Heinemann.

Routman, Regie. 2018. *Literacy Essentials: Engagement, Excellence, and Equity for All Learners.* Portland, ME: Stenhouse Publishers.

Routman, Regie. 2014. *Read, Write, Lead: Breakthrough Strategies for Schoolwide Literacy Success.* Alexandria, VA: ASCD.

Scarborough, H.S. (2001). "Connecting early language and literacy to later reading (dis)abilities: Evidence, theory, and practice." In S. Neuman & D. Dickinson (Eds.), *Handbook of Early Literacy Research* (pp. 97–110). New York, NY: Guilford Press.

Seidenberg, Mark. 2017. *Language at the Speed of Sight: How We Read, Why So Many Can't, and What Can Be Done About It.* New York, NY: Basic Books.

Stern, Julie. 2018. *Tools for Teaching Conceptual Understanding: Harnessing Natural Curiosity for Learning That Transfers.* Thousand Oaks, CA: Corwin.

Wexler, Natalie. 2019. *The Knowledge Gap: The Hidden Cause of America's Broken Education System—And How to Fix It.* New York, NY: Avery.

Willingham, Daniel T. 2017. *The Reading Mind: A Cognitive Approach to Understanding How the Mind Reads.* San Francisco, CA: Jossey-Bass.

Willms, Heather and Giacinta Alberti. 2022. *This Is How We Teach Reading… And It's Working!: The What, Why, and How of Teaching Phonics in K-3 Classrooms.* Markham, ON: Pembroke Publishers.

Wolf, Maryanne. 2007. *Proust and the Squid: The Story and Science of the Reading Brain.* New York, NY: HarperCollins Publishers.

Wolf, Maryanne. 2018. *Reader, Come Home: The Reading Brain in a Digital World.* New York, NY: HarperCollins Publishers.

Index